This book is to be returned on or before
the last date stamped below.

301103

PROJECTS

D1347029

Library Services
Victoria Buildings
Queen Street
Falkirk
FK2 7AF

Falkirk Council

297
EGA

Andrew Egan

Heinemann
LIBRARY

www.heinemann.co.uk/library
Visit our website to find out more
information about **Heinemann
Library** books.

To order:
📞 Phone 44 (0) 1865 888066
📠 Send a fax to 44 (0) 1865 314091
 Visit the Heinemann Bookshop at
www.heinemann.co.uk/library to
browse our catalogue and order online.

For Olivia

Heinemann Library
Halley Court, Jordan Hill, Oxford, OX2 8EJ
Part of Harcourt Limited

Heinemann is the registered trademark of
Harcourt Education Limited

Text © Andrew Egan, 2002

First published in 2002

ISBN 0 431 14987 9 (hardback)
06 05 04 03 02
10 9 8 7 6 5 4 3 2 1

ISBN 0 431 14994 1 (paperback)
07 06 05 04 03
10 9 8 7 6 5 4 3 2 1

All rights reserved

Apart from any fair dealing for the purposes of research
or private study, or criticism or review as permitted
under the terms of the UK Copyright, Designs and
Patents Act, 1988, this publication may not be
reproduced, stored or transmitted, in any form or by any
means, without the prior permission in writing of the
publishers, or in the case of reprographic reproduction
only in accordance with the terms of the licences issued
by the Copyright Licensing Agency in the UK, or in
accordance with the terms of licences issued by the
appropriate Reproduction Rights Organization outside
the UK. Enquiries concerning reproduction outside the
terms stated here should be sent to the publishers at the
address printed on this page.

British Library Cataloguing in Publication Data
A catalogue record for this book is available from the
British Library

Picture research by Jennifer Johnson
Designed and typeset by Artistix, Thame, Oxon
Printed and bound in Spain by Edelvive

Acknowledgements
The author would like to thank Imam Aurangzeb Khan
for all the wise words and kind prayers that have helped
to make this book possible.

The publishers would like to thank the following for
permission to use photographs:

Andes Press Agency/Carlos Reyes-Mayer, p. 45; Andes
Press Agency/D&C Hill, p. 52; Andrew Egan, p. 8;
Hutchison Picture Library/Edward Parker, p. 44;
Hutchison Picture Library/Nigel Smith, p. 42; Hutchison
Picture Library/Titus Moser, p. 15; Panos Pictures/Jeremy
Hartley, pp. 47 and 48; Panos Pictures/Penny Tweedie,
p. 51; Rex Features/Eastlight Vienna, p. 55; Science Photo
Library/Celestial Image Co., p. 57; Science Photo
Library/ESA/Photo Library International, p. 40; Science
Photo Library/Peter Menzel, p. 56. All other photographs
supplied by Peter Sanders.

The publishers have made every effort to contact
copyright holders. However, if any material has been
incorrectly acknowledged, the publishers would be
pleased to correct this at the earliest opportunity.

Tel: 01865 888058 www.heinemann.co.uk

Contents

An introduction to Islam

In this section you will:

- develop an understanding of the nature and importance of faith and trust
- think about the ways in which Islam seeks to strengthen faith in Allah
- explore and understand the aims of Islam.

Standing before Allah in prayer

Faith and trust

The religion of **Islam**, like all religions, is based on **belief**. To believe in something means that you have no doubt at all, even if there is very little evidence to back up your belief.

To believe in something requires **faith** and **trust**. Faith is often seen as the courage to accept the challenges of belief and trust as the certainty that you won't be let down.

The people who follow Islam are called **Muslims**. The worldwide community of Muslims is known as the **ummah**. The ummah shows Islam to be one great family, different in local culture and custom, but still united as one family before Allah.

Allah

All Muslims have faith and trust in **Allah**, the Almighty God who created all things. For Muslims, Islam is more than just a series of beliefs, it is a complete way of life. They believe that not only has Allah created all things but that Allah has also provided guidance to help all people live good lives. Therefore to be a true Muslim means to accept Allah as the one true God and to submit to His will.

Islam teaches that no one is superior to another except if one is more faithful to Allah. Islam aims at the development of an united human society on earth guided by the holy laws of Allah.

A Muslim family

The aims of Islam

Islam grants freedom of thought to all believers. It strives to free the soul from sin and wrong and to strengthen it with goodness and purity. This is so that people can live lives dedicated to doing their best in the eyes of Allah, on behalf of other people and for themselves. Islam also aims to free the human self from vanity and greed, from envy and tension, from fear and insecurity. Islam, through submission to Allah, seeks to free people from the worship of false gods and low desires, unfolding before them the beautiful horizons of goodness and excellence. Islam fills the heart with fear of Allah, the only God in this world as well as the hereafter.

Islam wants to see its followers as honest, dutiful, pious, kind-hearted, reliable and sincere; this is achieved by a system of worship and duties.

Muslims are certain of their faith because Allah has told people about Himself over the centuries through holy people known as **prophets**. This is called revelation as Allah has used prophets to reveal something of Himself to people. The **Qur'an**, the Muslim holy book, mentions by name 25 prophets of Allah beginning with **Adam (pbuh)** and finishing with **Muhammad** (pbuh).

To show deep respect to the prophets of Islam, Muslims will say 'peace be upon him' when mentioning a prophet by name. Throughout this book (pbuh) will appear as a sign of respect after the mention of the names of any of the prophets of Allah. For Muslims, the last and greatest of the prophets was Muhammad (pbuh) to whom Allah revealed the Qur'an, His final message for the guidance of all.

Faith and trust – necessities of life

When you think about it, faith and trust are essential for our lives to function normally. We trust the electrical equipment in our homes, the cars and buses we ride on and, in particular, we trust the people around us. Our families and friends are important to us, but so are doctors, dentists, teachers, and police, fire and rescue services. We trust them all. For example, no one demands to see proof of a doctor's qualifications during a consultation or operation; we trust them.

Trust is therefore a very important part of human life. Without it, we would hardly get anything done because so much time would be spent doubting and questioning everything.

The only things that can be seen as reliable are mathematical ideas, such as $2 + 2 = 4$. This is a fact and cannot be disputed. However, such a fact is of no use to us should we need to see the dentist or receive first aid. It is our experience that informs most of our judgements. If we have a good experience of something or someone, then we are most likely to trust it or them.

It is in this way that Muslims trust Allah and have faith in Him as their God. Their experience of the world that Allah has made gives Muslims cause to trust that Allah is a powerful and loving God, and they have faith that He will care for His people.

The prophet Muhammad (pbuh)

In this section you will:

● find out about the vocation/calling of the prophet Muhammad (pbuh)

● begin to understand the nature of the message Muhammad (pbuh) was to convey to the people of Makkah

● explore the idea of vocation and what this might mean to all Muslims.

Muhammad's (pbuh) childhood

The prophet **Muhammad** (**pbuh**) was born in **Makkah** in 569 CE. Makkah is now in the modern country of Saudi Arabia.

By the time he was eight, his parents and grandparents were dead. He went into the care of his uncle, **Abu Talib**, a man who was kind and generous. Abu Talib travelled the region meeting many different people and doing business with them. Muhammad (pbuh) would often accompany his uncle on his business journeys.

The prophet of Islam

The people of Makkah were very superstitious and had little understanding of who **Allah** was, so they put their faith in statues and lucky charms. Muhammad (pbuh) was not like the others. He was a man of deep faith and prayed regularly. Gradually his spiritual meditation grew deeper and deeper. He would often isolate himself in a cave on **Jabal-un-Nur** (the Mountain of Light). There he would pray and meditate and share what little food he had with passers-by.

When he was 40 years old Muhammad (pbuh) was meditating one night when suddenly the Angel **Jibril** appeared before him in the cave.

The **Angel** told him that Allah had chosen him as His Final Messenger to all mankind. The Angel told him to recite (read out loud) the words on the cloth he was carrying and Muhammad (pbuh), although he could not read before that night, recited the following verses:

'In the name of Allah, Most Gracious, Most Merciful.
Recite! (read aloud): In the name of your Lord Who has created;
He has Created man from a clot.
Recite! And your Lord is Most Generous.
Who taught by the pen,
He has taught man that which he knew not.'

Qur'an, **surah** 96: 1–5

Muhammad (pbuh) was overawed by this incident and returned home dazed. He told **Khadijah**, his wife, what had happened to him. Muhammad thought that some evil spirit might be involved. Khadijah consoled him, saying that unlike most of the people of Makkah, he had always been generous and kind and assured him that Allah would protect him against all evil.

Muhammad's (pbuh) marriage to Khadijah was important as it provided him with a firm base of love and companionship upon which to build the mission to which Allah had called him. Without the faith and trust of his most loyal partner, his task would have been all the more difficult. Soon, another revelation directed him to warn people against evil, to encourage them to worship no other gods but Allah and to give up everything that could displease Allah:

'O you enveloped in garments,
Arise and warn!
And magnify your Lord
And purify your garments and keep away from idols.
And give not a thing in order to have more
And be patient for the sake of your Lord.'

Qur'an, surah 74: 1–7

Another revelation warned him to proclaim his mission openly:

'Proclaim openly that which you are
    commanded, and
Turn away from the idolaters.
Truly We will suffice you against the scoffers.'

Qur'an, surah 15: 94–5

It was essential that the people of Makkah heard and accepted the will of Allah, changed their ways and led better lives. It was Muhammad's (pbuh) task to ensure this happened.

The chain of revelations from Allah continued until the last one came 23 years after the first:

'This day, I have perfected your religion for you and completed My Favour upon you and have chosen for you Islam as your religion.'

Qur'an, surah 5: 3

After Muhammad's (pbuh) death all the revelations that he had received from Allah were written down as the **Qur'an**, the holy book of **Islam**.

The cave above Makkah

Muhammad's (pbuh) vocation

Muslims believe that Muhammad (pbuh) received a vocation from Allah. This vocation came in the form of a calling to go out to the people of Makkah and tell them to change their ways. Allah told Muhammad (pbuh) to tell the people that they should stop drinking, swearing and acting violently. Instead, they should live peacefully and respectfully together.

It was obvious that this was not going to be easy. However, Muhammad (pbuh) stuck to his task because of his deep faith and trust in Allah.

The vocation of every Muslim

Muslims believe that everyone has the potential to receive a vocation from Allah. It is true that not all callings are likely to be as dramatic as the one that Muhammad (pbuh) received, but all people do have the potential. This is because all the good aspects of human life are seen as aspects of Allah's love and creating power. For example, Islam teaches that all people have a calling to work hard, whether at school, in a job or around the house. We are to develop our talents and skills so that they may reflect the glory of Allah who gave them. Similarly, Allah calls all people to marry and raise families who know and love Him and follows His commandments.

The prophets

In this section you will:

- explore the essential characteristics of a prophet
- understand the importance of prophethood in Islam
- explore the significance of 'Isa (Jesus – pbuh) on the Islamic faith.

The messengers of Allah

Understanding the importance of prophethood is essential for a complete understanding of **Islam**. **Muslims** believe that **Muhammad** (**pbuh**) was the last of all the **prophets** of **Allah**.

The word 'prophethood' comes from the Arabic word '**risalah**', which means 'message'. In this case it means the communication of important news. Muslims believe that a prophet is someone who is sent by Allah to convey His message to other people.

Prophethood is not something that can be acquired by an individual's personal effort or devotion to Allah. It is Allah's special gift which He gives to a human being. There is no human involvement in His decision-making. Allah decides who is fit to be a prophet.

In the **Qur'an** this calling from Allah is called **istjfaa**, which means the selection of the best people. Muslims believe that the prophets were not like other people – they were born to be prophets and had qualities that no other human beings can have.

The message

'A prophet never speaks on his own accord
Nor does he speak of (his own) desire. It is only a Revelation revealed (by Allah).'

Qur'an, **surah** 53: 3–4

Islamic name	Biblical name
1 Ādam	Adam
2 Idrīs	Enoch
3 Noh	Noah
4 Had	——
5 Sālih	——
6 Ibrāhim	Abraham
7 Isma'il	Ishmael
8 Ishāq	Isaac
9 Lot	Lot
10 Ya'qūb	Jacob
11 Yūsuf	Joseph
12 Shu'aib	——
13 Ayyūb	Job
14 Musā	Moses
15 Hārūn	Aaron
16 Dhul-Kifl	Ezekiel
17 Dāwūd	David
18 Suleimān	Solomon
19 Ilyās	Elias
20 Al Yasa'	Elisha
21 Yūnas	Jonah
22 Zakaryah	Zechariah
23 Yahyā	John
24 'Isā	Jesus
25 Muhammad	——
(Peace be upon them all)	

The prophets of Islam

This means that Allah's message cannot be influenced by the personal thoughts or desires of a prophet. The word of Allah always remains undiluted in the hands of the prophet, while this is not possible in the case of an ordinary person. This is what distinguishes him from other human beings.

Examples of prophetic teaching include:

'He is not a believer who eats his fill while his neighbour remains hungry by his side.'

Muhammad (pbuh)

'There are many who fast during the day and pray all night, but they gain nothing but hunger and sleeplessness.'

Muhammad (pbuh)

'I say to you love God and love your neighbour as you love yourself.'

'Isa – Jesus (pbuh)

'When you fast, wash your face and look happy, that your fasting may not be seen by men but by your Father who is in secret; and your Father who is in secret will reward you.'

'Isa – Jesus (pbuh)

'The Lord is in His holy temple, the Lord's throne is in heaven; the Lord is good, He loves good deeds; the upright shall see His face.'

Dawud – David (pbuh)

'The righteous has enough to satisfy his appetite, but the belly of the wicked suffers want.'

Suleiman – Solomon (pbuh)

The message is very clear. The commandments from Allah (The Lord – Judaism, God – Christianity) demand of every individual a real sense of duty both towards Allah and towards other people.

Allah's prophets

Muslims believe that over the centuries Allah has sent prophets to reveal to people something of His divine nature and purpose. Of all the prophets Muhammad (pbuh) is the most important because he was the bearer of Allah's final message for humankind. However, the other prophets are very important too. Amongst these prophets is 'Isa – Jesus (pbuh).

The prophet 'Isa – Jesus (pbuh)

Christians believe that 'Isa (pbuh) was God's son. They believe that at the end of his earthly ministry 'Isa (pbuh) was put to death, crucified by the Roman authorities, and that after three days he was brought to life again in the resurrection. Although 'Isa (pbuh) is an important prophet for them, Muslims disagree with this understanding of his nature.

Islam teaches that the birth of 'Isa (pbuh) was a miracle. His mother was the virgin Maryam and he was conceived by the command of Allah (surah 19: 17–21). 'Isa (pbuh) was called to be a prophet when he was 30 years old, and he worked as a prophet for three years (surah 19: 29–34). Allah gave him miraculous powers: he could heal the sick, give sight to the blind and make the dead come back to life.

Islam contends that 'Isa (pbuh) called people to obey Allah alone but that some of his followers were so impressed by him that they considered him to be a part of Allah, the son of Allah (surah 5: 116–117). Muslims believe this to be an incorrect understanding of the person and work of 'Isa. Allah is one and indivisible. Allah can have no son or daughter, and to make such a claim implies a partnership. Islam is very clear that Allah has no partners and to suggest that He has is a very grave sin (surah 5: 17, 19: 35).

The Qur'an teaches that the prophet 'Isa (pbuh) was not crucified. Rather, he was taken up into heaven by Allah and did not suffer a human death.

Muslim leadership and authority

In this section you will:

● discover something of the role of the imam in the Muslim community

● consider the important role played by learned people in the faith of Islam

● develop an understanding of prayer in Islam and learn about some Muslim prayers.

The role of the imam

Many world faiths depend on the work of local religious leaders to guide them in their spiritual development and to be available to advise or comfort them in particular times of crisis or need. For example, Jews may look to their rabbi or Christians to their priest at such times. Jewish rabbis and Christian priests are often paid for the work they do as the calling to serve God that they are following is their full time occupation. The role of the **imam** in the **Muslim** community is different.

Generally speaking, in **Islam** there are no paid religious leaders. The **Qur'an** is clear in stating that Islam should not try to attract people to serve **Allah** by the promise of financial rewards.

Imam Aurangzeb Khan

'Leading a community in prayer before Allah is an honour, and teaching the meaning and importance of the word of Allah a privilege; to be paid would add nothing.

'I trained for seven years to become an imam. The training involved full study of both the Qur'an and the **Hadiths**. I felt called to this through a sense of wanting to develop my own prayer life and dedication to Allah.
The honour of being asked to then help others is a great bonus. Allah has given all things, including all our feelings and emotions. One thing in particular that He has given is the ability to ask questions like who am I? where have I come from? and where am I going? in terms of my relationship with Allah. I am a child of Allah and as such I want to grow closer to Him, fully engaged in His service.

'I see my main task as being there to help others to maintain their prayer life. For me my prayer life is rather like owning a car, if you look after it and service it regularly, it will serve you well. So it is with prayer, looked after well your prayer life will flourish and serve you well for life.'

Imam Aurangzeb Khan

Although it is rare, Muslim scholars have stated that in certain circumstances where a man is dedicated and fully engaged in his work as an imam then he may receive payment.

The imam is usually chosen by the local Muslim community that he is to serve. Any Muslim of good character can be an imam providing he:

● has a good knowledge of Islam

● is respected and held in high regard by fellow Muslims

● has studied the Qur'an, the holy book of Islam and the Hadiths, the sayings of the prophet Muhammad (pbuh) in Arabic and understands them well

An imam leading worship in a mosque

● is known for his faithfulness to and love of Allah and his ability to make wise decisions based upon good judgement.

Leading prayers

The main role of the imam is to lead the prayers at the **mosque** (the local centre of Muslim worship) in his community. Before the Friday lunchtime prayers (the most important prayers of the week) the imam will give two short talks or sermons called the **khutbah**. These sermons will usually involve an explanation of verses of the Qur'an or else a consideration of the important relevance of the Hadiths for Muslims today.

Similarly, it is the imam who will often lead prayers and read a sermon at a Muslim marriage or funeral and who will take a leading role in the work of the **madrasah** or school at the mosque where young Muslims will go to study Islam and in particular to study the Qur'an and to learn Arabic.

It is essential to remember that the imam is not a leader of Muslims. Islam is a faith that allows all its followers the space to find and to worship Allah for themselves. No Muslim, however learned or pious, would ever feel it right to tell another what to do or how to live their lives, because ultimately we are all answerable to Allah alone as individuals. The imam will, however, always encourage all in his community to live their lives in accordance with Islamic teachings.

Some Muslim prayers

After leading the community in prayer at the mosque, the imam will often make his own personal prayers to Allah. Often, the opportunity will be taken to ask Allah for forgiveness and mercy for all the times His high expectations have not been met.

The concept of Allah as a merciful and compassionate God is very powerful. Despite being hurt by human arrogance and sinfulness, Allah will always grant forgiveness and another chance to all those who call upon Him.

'In fact there is no real need to say such prayers out loud. Allah knows all the secrets of every heart and so will have forgiven the person who is truly sorry even before they voice their prayer.'

Imam Aurangzeb Khan

Such prayers can be said either in Arabic (the language of the Qur'an) or in the individual's own language.

'O our Lord, grant us good in this world and good in the next world, save us from the punishment of hell.'

'O Allah, you are the source of peace and from you comes peace, you are most highly exalted, O lord of majesty and honour.'

'O Allah, forgive me and my parents and my teachers and all believing men and women and all Muslim men and women in your great mercy. O most merciful lord, you have all mercy.'

'Our lord, we have wronged ourselves. Forgive us and have mercy on us. Without you we can not win through.'

Muslim beliefs

In this section you will:

- find out about the most important Muslim beliefs
- learn about the five pillars of Islam which support Muslims.

Muslims believe that the religion of **Islam**, revealed to the **prophet Muhammad (pbuh)**, is the true religion of **Allah**, the one true God. The most fundamental **beliefs** of Islam are:

1. in Allah
2. in the will of Allah (predestination)
3. in the angels of Allah
4. in the books of Allah
5. in the messengers (prophets) of Allah
6. in the day of judgement
7. in life after death.

These seven fundamental beliefs can be placed into three broader groups:

1. **tawhid** – the oneness of Allah
2. **risalah** – the work and message of the prophets
3. **akhirah** – life after death.

Tawhid, risalah and akhirah summarize the whole of the Muslim way of life.

Tawhid

Tawhid means the oneness of Allah. It is the main part of the faith of Muslims and is expressed most beautifully in the **Qur'an**:

'Say, He is Allah, the One. Allah is the self sufficient master Whom all creatures need. He begets not nor was begotten. And there is none co-equal or comparable to Him.'

Qur'an, **surah** 112

Tawhid means that everything on earth is created by Allah. It is Allah who is therefore the sustainer of the universe and the only source of human guidance.

'It is Allah alone who has created all things, given all things, is all things. We would have nothing, be nothing without Allah.'

Mariah, aged 14

Risalah

Risalah refers to the important role played by the prophets in Islam.

'Allah sent among them a messenger from among themselves, reciting unto them His Verses, and purifying them, and instructing them in the book and wisdom.'

Qur'an, surah 3: 164

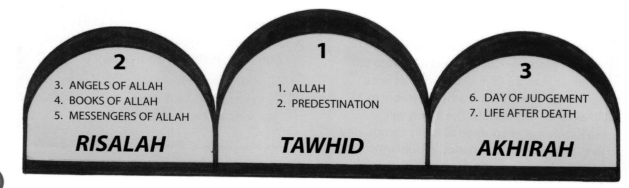

2
3. ANGELS OF ALLAH
4. BOOKS OF ALLAH
5. MESSENGERS OF ALLAH

RISALAH

1
1. ALLAH
2. PREDESTINATION

TAWHID

3
6. DAY OF JUDGEMENT
7. LIFE AFTER DEATH

AKHIRAH

This means quite simply that:

'Allah has sent His messenger with … the religion of truth, to make it victorious.'

Qur'an, surah 61: 9

'Allah wants to guide us when we go wrong or help us when we misunderstand. For me, the prophets are those specially chosen by Allah to guide and help us to know Allah better and to understand what Allah wants.'

Mudassir, aged 15

Akhirah

Akhirah refers to the important Muslim belief in a life after death that can be enjoyed by all believers. Allah's message is:

'Did you think that We had created you in play and that you would not be brought back to us?'

Qur'an, surah 23: 115

'And those who disbelieve say "when we have become dust we and our fathers, shall we really be brought forth again?"'

Qur'an, surah 27: 67

This is because those who disbelieve deny that there is life after death. For Muslims, however, the answer to the question 'is there life after death' is a definite 'yes', because Allah has promised a glorious afterlife and Allah never breaks His promises.

'Life does not simply begin when we are physically born and end when we physically die. Really our lives belonging to Allah begin before physical birth and continue after physical death. This is really simple to understand when you think of every human life as belonging to Allah.'

Mudassir, aged 15

In effect, then, Islam teaches that human life is one eternal life made up of two parts, life before and life after death. Muslims believe that the spirit of life that Allah has breathed into everyone is raised by Allah, from death to the afterlife. It is to be here, in the afterlife, that Allah will call all to account for themselves and judge them according to the way they have led their lives on earth. Those who have led good lives, it is said, will enter paradise with Allah and those who have led bad, wicked lives will be punished.

The duty to worship Allah

There are five important parts to Muslim worship. Together they could be said to support or 'hold up' what it means to be a Muslim. They are known as the five pillars of Islam.

The first pillar is **shahadah**, what every Muslim believes: that there is only one God – Allah – and that Muhammad (pbuh) is His prophet. It belongs at the very heart of every Muslim act of worship.

The second pillar is **salah**, prayer five times a day. This is the clearest evidence of the worship which Muslims offer to Allah.

The third pillar is **zakah**, giving money or 'alms' to people who are poor or needy. This is a powerful form of worship because through helping other people Allah is being served.

The fourth pillar is **sawm**, fasting (going without food) during the month of Ramadan. Fasting is a form of worship because it helps to focus hearts and minds on Allah and the needs of others.

The fifth pillar is **Hajj**, pilgrimage to Makkah. This is the most holy of all places for Muslims.

Allah

In this section you will:

- develop an understanding of the most important characteristics of Allah
- explore the meaning of blasphemy in Islam
- read and think about some of the 99 names for Allah.

Muslim beliefs about Allah

Some people seem to pass their entire lives without ever thinking about the reason for their existence, or whether there is any point to their lives, or any goal to be aimed for. Many think there is a universe and that is all there is. They believe their lives are simply a chain of events until they die.

Muslims, however, say it is impossible for anything to have being or purpose without God. To recognize that **Allah** does exist and is the beginning and end of all things is essential to the **faith** of **Islam**.

Muslims believe that Allah is one and at one with all things and that there is no other god except Him. This belief is called **tawhid**. The **prophet Muhammad** (**pbuh**) attacked all forms of **belief** in God which denied His oneness and unity.

The word 'Islam' means 'submission'. The way in which Muslims submit themselves to the will of Allah accurately reflects what Muslims believe about Allah and the way in which Allah expects them to live their lives. True Muslims would never put themselves and what they want first but reflect on what Allah would expect and obey His will.

Allah, the name of God

Shirk

Blasphemy means acting or speaking disrespectfully about God. The Arabic word **shirk** can be understood as describing a form of blasphemy.

Shirk can be thought of as the blasphemy of 'association', that is to say, to talk or act in any way which denies that Allah is Lord over everything by associating Him with someone or something else. Anyone who does this commits the most awful blasphemy. The name 'Allah' in Arabic – the language of the **Qur'an** – has no plural form, and is neither male nor female. Shirk, then, is either the worship of anything other than Allah, or the association of Allah with anything other than Allah.

Why do you think Muslims might feel the power of Allah is displayed in this sunrise?

12

Understanding Allah

Muslims often find it possible to understand Allah best in terms of the wonders of His creation. The whole universe is Allah's creation and everything in it belongs to Allah and is dependent on Allah.

'Allah alone created all things, gave all things, is all things. Allah is like nothing or no one, Allah is greater than anything we can ever hope to imagine, it's pointless and wrong to ever try to bring Allah down to our level. The love and power of Allah is a beautiful mystery, I'm happy with that.'

Mariah, aged 14

One of the best ways of understanding the power of Allah in the universe is through an appreciation of the light that Allah has provided for the world. The following quotations show how important the gift of light is for Muslims.

'Allah will give you a Light by which you will walk.'

Qur'an, **surah** 57: 28

'O Lord! Illuminate my heart with light, my sight with light and my hearing with light. Let there be light on my right hand and on my left and light behind me and light going before me.'

A prayer of Muhammad (pbuh)

'O God, who knows the innermost secrets of our hearts – lead us out of the darkness into the light.'

A prayer of Muhammad (pbuh)

Names of Allah

Muslims have 99 names for Allah, which express His nature in all its diversity. Here are the first 33 of Allah's names:

God
The Compassionate
The Merciful
The King
The Holy
The Peace
The One with Faith
The Protector
The Mighty
The Repairer
The Imperious
The Creator
The Maker
The Fashioner
The Forgiver
The Dominant
The Bestower
The Provider
The Opener
The Knower
The Contractor
The Expander
The Humbler
The Exalter
The Honourer
The Abaser
The Hearer
The Seer
The Judge
The Just
The Subtle
The Aware
The Gentle

Thinking about Allah

In this section you will:

● think about ways in which Muslims talk about Allah

● reflect on a parable which explains what Muslims mean when they talk of their faith in Allah.

Madrasah – 'Muslim children learning ways to effectively express their beliefs about Allah'

The nature of the universe

For some people understanding the nature of **Allah** (God) is difficult. People have traditionally tended to think of Allah as being 'up there'

A 3-storey depiction of the universe

inhabiting a wonderful place called Heaven, surrounded by His **angels** and all the good people who have died and gone to glory. The opposite can be said for **Shaytan** (the Devil) who dwells far beneath the earth in Hell, surrounded by the forces of evil and all the wicked people who are being punished for their sins after their death. This means that we as human beings inhabit a sort of middle ground, called earth.

However, we now know scientifically that the universe in which we live is not like that. We know from all the many space missions that have been launched that the sky does not provide a home for Allah, but rather, by its many layers, gives protection for the earth from the sun's harmful rays. We also now know that the earth is round, so Hell cannot be below the earth, as that would actually be sky for people living on the other side of the world.

The nature of Allah

Muslims prefer to talk of Allah as being one absolute power. The absolute power of Allah is plain for all to see. The laws of nature, the order of the universe and the beauty of creation reflect a little of Allah but are not Allah. Allah is above and beyond the universe, unlimited by time and space. He knows everything and is the all-powerful creator and controller of all things.

The beauty of Allah's creation

To make talking of Allah easier, Muslims often refer to Allah as 'He' or things belonging to Allah as 'His'. This is not to suggest that Allah is male or to deny that Allah is female, but it enables human beings, who can only have a limited understanding of Allah and a limited vocabulary, an opportunity to express feelings, prayer and other forms of worship.

The 99 names of Allah

Understanding Allah – a parable

The concept of God is not an easy one to either understand or explain. This parable, although not **Islamic** in origin, can help us to understand what Muslims mean when they talk of their faith and trust in Allah.

Two explorers are walking through the jungle when they come to a clearing. In the clearing there are many flowers growing, and also many weeds.

The first explorer says, 'Some gardener must tend this spot.' The other disagrees: 'There is no gardener.' So they pitch their tents and set about watching, but no gardener is ever seen.

'But perhaps he is an invisible gardener,' says the first explorer. So they set up barbed wire, an electric fence and a patrol with bloodhounds. But there are no shrieks to suggest that an intruder has received an electric shock, and no movements whatsoever to betray an invisible climber. The bloodhounds are silent – they have no scent of this invisible gardener.

'But,' says the first explorer, 'perhaps there is an invisible, intangible, gardener; insensible to electric shocks. A gardener who has no scent and makes no sound – a gardener who comes secretly to tend the garden he loves.'

'Well,' says the second explorer, 'what now remains of your original assertion? Just how does your invisible, intangible, eternally elusive gardener differ from an imaginary gardener – or, indeed, no gardener at all?'

Signs and symbols

In this section you will:

- consider reasons why symbolic language is often an important part of religious belief and practice
- think about why religious language is sometimes difficult
- learn about the appropriateness of the star and crescent moon as symbols of Islam.

Muslims feel little need for symbols in their religion. However, as a reminder of the guidance **Allah** provides for His people, two very powerful symbols are often used in **Islam**.

The star and crescent moon

Islam began in the desert of Arabia amongst nomadic farmers who would travel by night, away from the searing heat of the sun's rays, in search of the best food and water for their animals. The moon would provide light through the darkness of the night and the stars gave fixed points which the people could use to navigate the vast desert. In just the same way, Muslims are happy to think of Allah as the great guiding light in their lives.

Islam teaches that Allah has revealed the truth through the **prophet Muhammad (pbuh)** as a guide for life, for all humanity, for all time. The star and crescent moon provide a reminder of both the permanence and the benefits of the Word and Will of Allah.

'Allah is the Spirit, the power behind all things, Allah is in all things, Allah is all things.'

Salim, aged 13

'I know that Allah loves all that He has made. Best of all Allah loves us so we return love in worship.'

Mariah, aged 14

'Allah is every mystery and every answer in the universe.'

Mudassir, aged 15

Religious language

The need for symbolic language in religion is important. When you think of it, we expect our language to cover a vast range of different jobs. Sometimes it may be used to portray feelings of love or other emotions. At other times it may be used to teach complex mathematics, comfort an upset child or negotiate a business deal. We require our language to cover a wide range of emotions and situations. Unfortunately, we only have a limited vocabulary and so tend to use the same word for a variety of meanings. For example the word 'love':

1. Olivia loves strawberries.
2. Olivia loves her Mum and Dad.
3. Olivia loves her cuddly Teddy Bear.

It is not easy to gain an exact understanding of a word as popular as 'love' as it can mean different things to different people at different times.

When people want to talk about God they have to use the same words that are commonly used in everyday language. There is a problem therefore, in what is meant exactly by the claims 'God is good' or 'God loves us'. Possible answers to this problem might be to say that:

1 a religious language, talk about God, is used in a special way as it is describing something unique

b religious language is used in a very specific sense and should not be confused with the everyday language of the home, school and playground

2 it is because of the difficulties presented by the use of everyday words to express religious truths that:

a symbols – pictures with a powerful meaning

b analogies, 'symbolic pictures' – 'drawn' with words describing what something could be said to be like. For example, 'Allah's love for us is like the love of a parent for their child'

c myths – stories which share with the reader important religious truths

are used widely by people of many religions to express their beliefs about God.

Allah in the Qur'an

Here are a further selection of the names of Allah. Together they help Muslims to understand something of the nature of Allah.

The Mighty
The Forgiving
The Grateful
The Lofty
The Great
The Guardian
The Nourisher
The Light
The Guide
The Gatherer
The Hidden
The First
The Last
The Truth
The Strong
The One
The Loving
The Wise

Decoration in Islam

Muslims have developed a beautiful style of art to decorate mosques and editions of the Qur'an, using a variety of geometric designs and patterns. Here is an example of this type of decoration:

Part of surah 112 of the Qur'an

Worship – Shahadah

In this section you will:

● learn about the importance of worshipping Allah for every Muslim

● understand the importance of shahadah in the worship of Allah

● gain an understanding of the adhan – the Muslim call to prayer.

The five pillars of Islam

The most important duty of every **Muslim** is to worship **Allah**. The word 'worship' in English comes from a very old word meaning 'to give worth'. It is clear in this case that Allah is 'worth' a great deal of praise and adoration, indeed worthy of and demanding the complete submission of His people to His will.

Worshipping Allah, then, demands the total obedience of every Muslim to follow His commands and to do His will. The Arabic word for such obedience in worship is **ibadah**. Ibadah comes from the Arabic word **abd**, which means servant or slave. A servant or slave is someone who is completely obedient to their master. Every Muslim would happily admit that Allah alone is their Lord and master.

'It is then as Allah's servant or slave that a Muslim tries to live their life. In doing so every aspect of their life is the worship of Allah, from working to relaxing, from praying to raising a family.'

Imam Aurangzeb Khan

There are five duties that are of fundamental importance in Muslim worship. These five duties, often referred to as 'pillars', include:

1 **shahadah** – the declaration of faith in Allah

2 **salah** – prayer five times each day

3 **zakah** – the giving of money for the poor

4 **sawm** – fasting during the month of Ramadan

5 **Hajj** – pilgrimage to **Makkah** at least once in a lifetime.

Shahadah

The first and most important duty of every Muslim is to declare their faith in Allah. **Islam** teaches that to make this declaration a person must proclaim with their lips and believe in their heart:

'Ash hadu an laa ilaha il-allahu wa Ash hada anna Muhammadar abduhu wa rasulu.'
('I believe there is no god but Allah; and I believe that Muhammad is the servant and messenger of Allah.')

It is clear that the first part of this declaration has two aspects, one positive and one negative. 'There is no other god' is the negative aspect, 'but Allah' the positive aspect affirming the truth and certainty of Allah.

The saying of these Arabic words is called shahadah, the declaration of faith. The shahadah is repeated by Muslims every day as they wake up and just before sleeping. The words form the heart of the Muslim call to prayer (the **adhan**), used to summon Muslims to prayer five times each day. The call to prayer is also the first words whispered into the ear of a new born baby. Similarly, the last words uttered by a Muslim before dying should ideally be the **Kalimah Tayyibah**, which like the call to prayer summarizes the Muslim belief that Allah is one and that **Muhammad (pbuh)** is his servant and messenger.

'The message of Islam is very important and very simple, because if Allah wants you to do something He lets you know. The Prophet has taught that Allah wants worship, our way of thanking Him for everything. This worship is in the five pillars. You make a choice, to follow and worship Allah or not. It's a way of choosing either Heaven (being with Allah) or Hell (being separated from Allah).

'Islam means to submit yourself, give in to Allah. Worshipping Allah involves time and commitment throughout your life. It is right to worship, look at everything we have been given by Allah.'

Shamira, aged 13

The adhan

Islam encourages Muslims to say their compulsory prayers in the **mosque** whenever possible. To call Muslims to prayer, the prophet Muhammad (pbuh) introduced the adhan – the call to prayer. The person who recites the adhan is called the mu'adhin. He stands in the **minaret** of the mosque, faces Makkah, raises his hands to his ears and calls out a special form of words.

The words of the adhan

During the call to prayer, the Mu'adhin will call out these words:

Allahu Akbar
Allahu Akbar
Allahu Akbar
Allahu Akbar
Ash hadu an laa ilaha il-allahu
Ash hadu an laa ilaha il-allahu
Ash hada anna Muhammadar abduhu wa
    rasulu
Ash hada anna Muhammadar abduhu wa
    rasulu
Hayya 'alas salah
Hayya 'alas salah
Hayya 'alal falah
Hayya 'alal falah
Allahu Akbar
Allahu Akbar
Laa ilaha il-allahu

This may be translated as:

Allah is the greatest
Allah is the greatest
Allah is the greatest
Allah is the greatest
I bear witness that there is no god but
    Allah
I bear witness that there is no god but
    Allah
I bear witness that Muhammad is Allah's
    messenger
I bear witness that Muhammad is Allah's
    messenger
Rush to prayer
Rush to prayer
Rush to success
Rush to success
Allah is the greatest
Allah is the greatest
There is no god but Allah

Worship – Salah 1

In this section you will:

● develop an understanding of the importance of prayer in the lives of Muslims

● think about the ways in which Muslims believe prayer can bring individuals closer to Allah

● consider ways in which prayer can help to build up and strengthen whole communities.

Salah

Salah is one of the most important of the five basic duties of **Islam** as it requires **Muslims** to focus their hearts and minds completely on **Allah** in prayer five times every day. The way in which Muslims pray and the times at which prayers are said are laid down in the **Qur'an**. Muslims can come closer to Allah by performing salah regularly, correctly and with a full understanding of its significance and meaning.

Muslims believe that the purpose of human creation is to worship Allah. Allah declares in the Qur'an:

'And I created not … mankind except that they worship me.'

Qur'an, **surah** 51: 56

Therefore, Muslims believe that whatever we do we must bear in mind that we are doing it for Allah's sake. Only then can we expect to gain any benefit from the performance of salah.

'Salah is important for a number of reasons:

● it brings men and women closer to Allah

● it keeps human beings away from forbidden activities

Muslims at prayer

● it is designed to control evil desires and passions

● it purifies the heart, develops the mind and comforts the soul

● it is a constant reminder of Allah and His greatness

● it develops discipline and will power

● it shows that Islam is one universal family – the ummah

● it is a means of cleanliness, purity and punctuality

● it develops gratitude, humility and refinement

● it is a sign of total obedience to the will of Allah.

Similarly, the Qur'an teaches that if your salah does not improve the way in which you conduct your life, you must think seriously and find out where you are going wrong.'

Imam Aurangzeb Khan

The times of salah

Salah is performed five times every day at special times:

1 Salat-ul-Fajr – between first light and sunrise

2 Salat-ul-Zuhr – just after the sun has left its highest point in the sky

3 Salat-ul-Asr – between mid-afternoon and sunset

4 Salat-ul-Maghrib – between sunset and darkness

5 Salat-ul-Isha – between darkness and dawn.

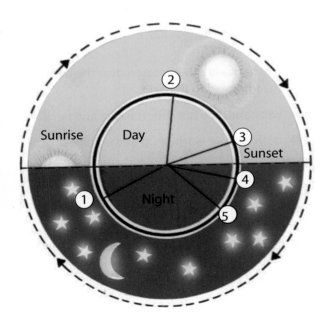

Rak'ahs

Salah is performed by following a strict ritual of set movements and prayers. A rak'ah is a sequence of movements. Two rak'ahs are repeated at Salat-ul-Fajr; four at Salat-ul-Zuhr and Salat-ul-Asr; three at Salat-ul-Maghrib; and four at Salat-ul-Isha. At each rak'ah, set prayers are repeated.

Eight positions make up a rak'ah:

1 standing up straight

2 raising your hands to your ears

3 placing your right hand on your left hand just below your navel or on your chest

4 bowing down

5 placing your hands on your knees

6 prostrating yourself with your forehead, nose, palms of your hands and knees touching the floor

7 kneeling upright

8 whilst still kneeling, turning your face from left to right.

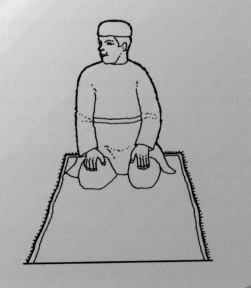

In this section you will:

● examine the preparations made by Muslims before they pray

● learn about the different types of prayer in Islam

● read and reflect upon the set prayers recited at salah.

Preparing for salah

'**Islam** requires **Muslims** to pray five times every day.

'Before we say **salah** we prepare ourselves. In order to focus our hearts and minds on **Allah**, before prayer we wash. This is called **wudu**. Wudu is compulsory and we can not make our salah without first making our wudu.

'Wudu, like salah, is written in the **Qur'an**. It requires the washing of different parts of our bodies, even if we are not very dirty, it is more of a spiritual washing as we prepare to stand before Allah.'

Imam Aurangzeb Khan

After entering into a meditative and prayerful frame of mind by dedicating the wudu that they are about to perform 'In the name of Allah, the most Merciful, the most Kind', Muslims follow a set pattern or ritual:

● the hands are washed up to the wrists three times

● the mouth is rinsed three times

● the nostrils are washed three times as is the tip of the nose

● the face is washed thoroughly three times

● both arms are washed up to the elbow three times

A Muslim performing wudu

● wet hands are then passed over the hair from the forehead to the neck

● wet hands are run over the ears and neck

● both feet are washed up to the ankles.

In addition to the daily salah obligations Muslims can also make their own private and personal prayers at any time. This type of prayer is called **du'a**. Du'a is an opportunity for every Muslim to bring before Allah their own individual concerns, for example, to pray for someone who is ill or in particular need. Du'a also provides the opportunity to meditate on the wonderful gifts Allah has given or to seek the strength of Allah to work hard in their religious duties and to become better people.

Du'a prayer

Therefore, different types of prayer can be included in the performance of du'a. These may include:

- adoration – praising Allah for all the wonderful things He has provided

- intercession – praying for the needs of others

- supplication – asking for the strength to overcome the temptations and pressures of the world and to grow in faith

- confession – saying sorry before Allah for the times when the temptations to sin have been too strong to resist.

Set prayers at salah

Set prayers are repeated at salah, accompanying the different positions which make up a rak'ah. It is very important for Muslims to follow the correct procedure. These are some of the prayers recited at salah.

'Allah is the greatest.'

'O Allah, glory and praise are for you, and blessed is your name, and exalted is your majesty: you alone are God.'

'I seek shelter in Allah from Shaytan.'

'In the name of Allah, the most merciful, the most kind.'

'Glory to you my Lord, the great.'

'Allah hears those who praise Him.'

'Praise to you, our Lord.'

'Glory to you my Lord, the highest.'

'Peace and mercy of Allah be upon you.'

The opening chapter of the Qur'an is always recited during salah, and a further passage is also selected and read out.

'All praise be to Allah,
the Lord of the Universe,
the Most Merciful, the Most Kind,
Master of the Day of Judgement.
You alone do we worship,
From you alone do we seek help.
Show us the next step
along the straight path
of those earning Your favour.
Keep us from the path of
those earning Your anger,
those who are going astray.'

(surah 1)

Worship – Sawm

In this section you will:

- understand the importance of fasting in the lives of Muslims
- think about ways in which fasting can strengthen people in faith as well as self-discipline
- learn about Islamic customs during the month of Ramadam.

Sawm

Sawm is the fourth pillar of **Islam**. Sawm means 'fasting' and all adult **Muslims** must fast from dawn to sunset every day of **Ramadan**, the ninth month of the Islamic calendar. In practice this means abstaining from eating, drinking, smoking and sexual relations during the hours of daylight. Travellers and those who are ill during Ramadan can put off not eating and drinking and make up for it later.

Sawm can develop self-control and help people to overcome selfishness, greed and laziness. It is in effect an annual opportunity to refresh and refocus the hearts and minds of Muslims in their worship of **Allah**.

By fasting, Muslims experience for themselves what it is like to have an empty stomach. This develops an empathy for all the poor and hungry people in the world. Fasting teaches Muslims to control the love of comfort, it also helps Muslims to control sexual desires. The **Qur'an** is clear in its teaching that eating, comfort and sex are three things which must be kept under control to behave effectively as Allah's servants:

'O you who believe! Fasting is prescribed for you as it was prescribed for those before you that you may become pious.'

Qur'an, **surah** 2: 183

A Muslim family breaking the fast

Fasting therefore is a sign of a truly obedient Muslim. The following actions, however, will break the fast:

1. deliberate eating or drinking

2. anything entering the body through the nose or mouth; this includes smoking

3. having any sexual relations.

Muslims are expected to make an extra effort to refrain from all immoral actions during the fast. They should not tell lies, break a promise or do anything deceitful.

The importance of sawm

The purpose of fasting is to make a Muslim able to control passions and desires, so that they become a person of good deeds and intentions. Similarly, fasting helps to develop an increased awareness of knowing what it is to go without, even for a little while, and to know hunger.

Exceptions to the rule

Although most Muslims can and will take part in fasting during Ramadan, there are sometimes unavoidable circumstances which mean that a person is unable to fast.

Very young children and the elderly are not expected to fast at all, and neither are women who are pregnant. If a Muslim is ill or is travelling during Ramadan, they are excused from fasting at that time, but are expected to make up for any missed days later.

At the end of Ramadan Muslims celebrate with a day of thanksgiving and happiness. The festival of **Id-ul-Fitr** is one of the great occasions for the Muslim community. On this day, Muslims offer special prayers at the **mosque** and thank Allah for all His blessings and mercies.

In addition to the compulsory fasting in Ramadan, Muslims may fast during other times of the year in order to refocus their hearts and minds on Allah.

Worship during Ramadan

The month of Ramadan is very important to Muslims. It is the month in which the Qur'an was first revealed to the **prophet Muhammad (pbuh)**.

During the month of Ramadan there is one night, which to Muslims is 'better than a thousand months' (Qur'an, surah 97: 3). This night is called Lailatul Qadr (the Night of Power) and it falls, according to the **Hadiths**, during the last ten days of the month. Many Muslims will pass this night in worship for as long as they can.

During the month of Ramadan additional prayers are repeated during **salah**. Tarawih is a special prayer through which Muslims attempt to recite as much of the Qur'an as possible. In many mosques, the whole of the Qur'an is recited through Tarawih prayer. Although it is usually recited by the congregation at the mosque, any Muslim who cannot attend the mosque should try to say Tarawih at home.

The mosque

In this section you will:

● find out about the Muslim place of worship

● think about the variety of ways in which the mosque is used by Muslims

● learn about ways in which Muslims decorate mosques with beautiful artwork.

The importance of the mosque

Muslims believe that **Allah** can be worshipped anywhere. The **prophet Muhammad (pbuh)** said:

'Wherever the hour of prayer overtakes you, you shall perform it. Because the whole earth has been turned into a mosque for me.'

Hadith

However, most Muslim communities will have a special building set aside for worship. These special buildings are called **mosques**. Mosques are important as they provide essential facilities for local people.

The main features of a mosque will include:

● the main prayer hall

● a separate section in which women pray

● a domed ceiling symbolizing the heavens above

● a **minaret**, a tower from which the community is called to prayer five times each day

● a **minbar**, a raised platform

● a **mihrab**, an archway showing the exact direction of Makkah.

In addition all mosques will have a supply of running water and separate rooms for women and men to place their shoes and to perform **wudu**.

Purpose-built mosques will often include offices and a number of rooms used for a variety of community needs, including:

● the mosque school where Muslim children can learn Arabic and more about their faith (the **madrasah**)

● for celebrations and parties

● as courts to hear cases relating to Islamic law.

Prayers are said five times every day at the mosque and are lead by the **imam**. At the main Friday prayers the imam will speak to the congregation from the minbar and give sermons explaining the meaning and importance of the Hadiths – the sayings of the prophet Muhammad (pbuh) or the **surahs** (chapters) of the **Qur'an**.

A mosque in Jeddah, Saudi Arabia

'The mosque is important as a focus of community prayer and learning, but for me not as important as my own family as the heart of my religion. The mosque is used regularly, every day, for people to go and pray to Allah and to learn new things, every day of your life. I have spent time at the mosque madrasah, for seven years, I started when I was four, and finished when I was ten.'

Shamira, aged 13

'The most important prayers at the mosque are the Friday lunchtime prayers. I think Friday is important as it shows Islam is separate from other religions, Judaism has Saturday and Christianity Sunday.'

Mudassir, aged 15

Inside the Niujie mosque, the oldest mosque in Beijing, China

Beautiful mosques

The mosque is the place where Muslims meet to stand together before Allah in prayer. Mosques are usually beautifully decorated. They may have richly coloured and patterned carpets and tiles, intricate stonework and chandeliers. However, the art and decorations which Muslims use in mosques are quite special.

Muhammad (pbuh) told his friends not to draw pictures of animals or people. He said that only Allah can make living beings, and it is wrong for human beings to try to imitate this.

Muhammad (pbuh) was also afraid that if people were to look at pictures or statues they might begin to worship them. Included in this were pictures or statues that were supposed to look like Allah or even Muhammad (pbuh). Worshipping such objects would be idol worship. Idol worship is wrong because the Qur'an teaches that Muslims should only worship that which is perfect. Only Allah is perfect.

Calligraphy

Muslim artists often draw beautiful flowers and plants. A highly developed art form in Islam, however, is calligraphy – the art of handwriting.

Calligraphy is often used to write out passages from the Qur'an. To write out the surahs in this way honours the words of Allah and is a wonderful privilege for the artist writing them.

Calligraphy is also used to create beautiful pictures, made up of letters, words from the Qur'an and prayers. It can be used on pottery and tiles, as well as on paper. It is in this way that all mosques have been decorated to the glory of Allah over the centuries.

Allah

Holy books – the Qur'an

In this section you will:

● find out about the importance of the Qur'an for Muslims

● learn about how Muslims treat their holy book with great respect.

The Qu'ran: the word of Allah

Islam teaches that human beings are the servants of **Allah**. This is seen as a great responsibility and so **Muslims** believe that they need guidance to carry out their duties as Allah's servants. Islam teaches that humans are unable to guide themselves because they have many weaknesses and are frail and short-sighted. Muslims believe only Allah is above all things and that it is He alone who has the power to give guidance that is valid for all times and places. Therefore, He has sent **prophets** and messengers to show humanity the right path in life. In addition to this, He has also given holy books for guidance.

'Allah's favours and blessings are countless. He provides us with all that we need. However, Allah's greatest favour is His guidance contained in the books of revelation. The pure, perfect and most useful knowledge comes only from Allah.'

Imam Aurangzeb Khan

The Qur'an – the word of Allah

The books of Allah

Muslims believe that Allah has inspired all the books which are mentioned in the **Qur'an**. These include the **Tawrah** (Torah) of **Musa** (Moses), the **Zabur** (Psalms) of **Dawud** (David), the **Injil** (Gospel) of **'Isa** (Jesus) and the Qur'an revealed to **Muhammad**. The Qur'an also mentions the **Sahifah of Ibrahim** (Scrolls of Abraham and Moses) (peace be upon them all).

Muslims believe that of all the divine books, only the Qur'an exists in its original, unchanged form. The Zabur, Tawrah and Injil were gradually altered after the death of the prophets to whom they were revealed, and their message changed and distorted. In effect they became a mixture of divine words with those of human beings.

Together all these writings go to make up one divine revelation, although Islam teaches that the Qur'an is most important for guiding human actions. Through these holy writings Allah has shown human beings something of His nature and has told them about the way in which He expects them to live their lives.

The message of the Qu'ran

'The message of the Qur'an is valid for all times and conditions. This is because the Qur'an contains the original messages revealed to Muhammad (**pbuh**). This message, passed from mouth to mouth and from heart to heart for over 1,400 years has enabled Muslims to know the true word of Allah.'

Imam Aurangzeb Khan

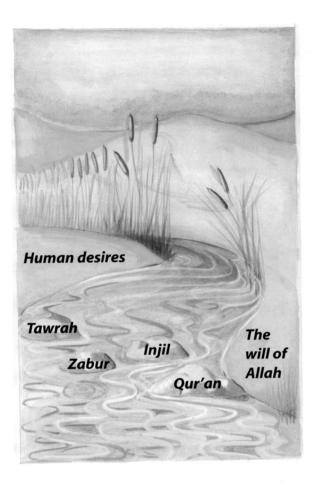

Human desires

Tawrah

Zabur

Injil

Qur'an

The will of Allah

Words from the Qur'an

Here are some passages taken from the Muslim holy books.

'God chooses for Himself whoever He pleases, and guides to Himself those who turn (to Him).'

(**surah** 42: 13)

'O people of the Book, you have no ground to stand on unless you stand fast by the Law, the Gospel, and all the revelation that has come to you from God.'

(surah 5: 68)

'This is My straight path, so follow it, and do not follow paths which will separate you from this path.'

(surah 6: 153)

'He will provide for you a light by which you will walk; He will forgive, for God always forgives and is most merciful.'

(surah 57: 28)

Respecting the Qur'an

Muslims treat the Qur'an with tremendous respect and honour. There are strict guidelines about how to do this.

The Qur'an is never allowed to touch the ground, and nothing should ever be placed on top of it. Before reading it, Muslims wash or bathe very carefully.

Muslims never handle the Qur'an unnecessarily. Whilst reading it, they do not speak, eat or drink. When they put it away, they keep it covered to protect it from dust.

Holy books – Hadiths

In this section you will:

● gain an understanding of the Hadiths and their importance in Islam

● understand the importance of Muhammad (pbuh) as an example to Muslims

● read about and reflect on the nature of truth in the Qur'an.

The importance of the Hadiths

Hadiths are important to **Muslims**. They are a collection of the words and teachings of the **prophet Muhammad (pbuh)** and are used by Muslims as a means of guidance and encouragement in their lives. This means that if ever faced with a difficult decision or dilemma, a Muslim can seek the help of **Allah** through the advice of the prophet Muhammad (pbuh) in the words of the Hadiths.

'No Muslim can underestimate the importance and significance of the Prophet, it was through him that Allah chose to finally reveal Himself both in the words of the Qur'an and in the divine messages revealed though the Hadiths.'

Imam Aurangzeb Khan

Hadiths are used by Muslims to help them live good lives. They provide guidance for living and can be applied to a wide range of social issues and situations.

Examples of Hadiths

1 'The best house among the Muslims is the house in which an orphan is well treated and the worst house among the Muslims is the house in which an orphan is badly treated.'

'One who tries to help the widow and the poor is like a warrior in the way of Allah.'

2 'Guarantee me six things and I shall assure you of paradise. When you speak, speak the truth, keep your promise, discharge your trust, guard your chastity and lower your gaze and withhold your hands from highhandedness.'

'Surely truth leads to virtue, and virtue leads to paradise.'

Muslims discussing the Hadiths

Two 'brother' Muslims

3 'Do not quarrel with your brother Muslim, nor jest with him nor make him a promise which you cannot keep.'

'Each of you is a mirror of his brother, if you see something wrong in your brother, you must tell him to get rid of it.'

'Believers are like the parts of a body to one another each part supporting the others.'

'None of you can be a believer unless he loves for his brother what he loves for himself.'

'A Muslim is he from whose tongue and hands other Muslims are safe.'

4 'Every good action is a charity and it is a good action to meet a friend with a smiling face.'

'There is a man who gives charity and he conceals it so much that his left hand does not know what his right hand spends.'

'Wealth does not come from abundance of goods but from a contented heart.'

5 'The best of you is he who has learnt the Qur'an and then taught it.'

'The seeking of knowledge is a must for every Muslim man and woman.'

'The learned men are the successors of the prophets. They leave behind knowledge as inheritance. One who inherits it obtains a great fortune.'

Understanding the Word of Allah

The teachings that Muslims follow have been revealed either through the Qur'an or through the Hadiths which were given to the prophet Muhammad (pbuh). Muslims believe that these are revelations from Allah about His nature and divine will.

However, the question may be asked how reliable this revelation is, given that it is human beings who have spread the message and have written it down. In other words, what does it mean to talk about Allah's revelation as 'true'?

Fundamentalist scholars are so sure of the **faith** and **trust** that they have in Allah that they are confident enough to say that every word of the Qur'an and the Hadiths is true – word for word. Even though they have been written down by human beings, fundamentalists believe that they are Allah's words and they have never been changed. They are true at all times and in all situations.

Liberal scholars view the revelations of Allah as true. However, rather than being true word for word, they see them as being true in the way in which poetry is true. Poetry is full of imagery and symbol, myth and metaphor, and so is true at different times for those who write it and for those who read it.

The Muslim understanding is that the Word of Allah is true, word for word. The absolute truth of the revelations of Allah are fundamental to the faith of Islam.

In this section you will:

- find out about the great Muslim festivals of Id-ul-Fitr and Id-ul-Adha
- consider the ways in which celebrating these festivals strengthen both personal faith and community spirit
- learn about the most important Muslim religious festivals.

Muslim festivals

There are two great **festivals** in **Islam**, **Id-ul-Fitr** which ends the fast of **Ramadan** and **Id-ul-Adha** which occurs during the month of **Hajj**, the time of pilgrimage to **Makkah**. Both are seen as occasions on which to give thanks to **Allah** for all His blessings and kindness.

Both festivals involve worship and care for others. The whole family (**ummah**) of Islam can feel very much together, celebrating these great festivals although separated around the world, enjoying a time with loved ones and sharing this good feeling by supporting all those who are poor or suffering in any way.

The requirements for feast days are simple:

- cleanliness – baths are taken and clean or new clothes worn

- prayer – **Muslims** come together in huge gatherings, to be as one. This is a very powerful example of the ummah – the Muslim community – as one

- thought for one's own family – presents are given, especially to children, special meals are served

- thought for others – **zakah** is collected and sent off, strangers are welcomed to share in hospitality.

After visiting the **mosque** on feast days, **Muslims** often go home by a different route from the one they took coming, in order to create the largest possible opportunity for meeting other Muslims, and spreading joy.

Id-ul-Fitr

Id-ul-Fitr is the celebration of the end of Ramadan, the month of fasting. The festival begins at the sight of the new moon that welcomes the start of the new month. Muslims celebrate by decorating their houses, giving and receiving cards and gifts and by attending special prayers at the mosque.

Zakah for Id-ul-Fitr is a special payment of a set amount, the equivalent of two meals. This should be given to the poor on behalf of each member of the family by every Muslim who is financially able to do this.

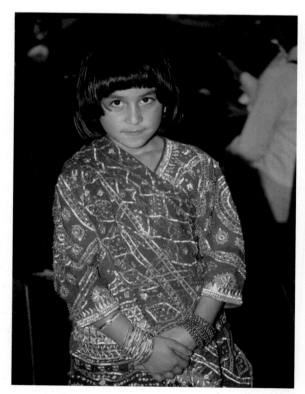

A Muslim dressed for Id

Id-ul-Adha

Id-ul-Adha is important for two reasons. Firstly, it marks the end of the Hajj, the pilgrimage to Makkah. Secondly, it recalls the faith in Allah displayed by the prophet **Ibrahim** (**pbuh**) when commanded to sacrifice his son **Isma'il** (pbuh).

As with the celebrations of Id-ul-Fitr, cards and gifts are given and received. However, the most important feature of the festival of Id-ul-Adha is the sacrifice of an animal to Allah. The sacrifice recalls the sacrifice of the ram that Allah provided for Ibrahim (pbuh) so he would not have to kill his son Isma'il (pbuh). Muslims may sacrifice sheep, goats, cows and camels. Muslim families enjoy a big meal using the meat from their sacrifice and share the remaining meat with the poor of the community or with friends and relatives.

'I enjoy celebrating Id because it's thanking Allah for the family and friends we have and sharing a happy time with them.'

Shamira, aged 13

Celebrating in the love of Allah

The Muslim festivals

Each month in the Muslim calendar follows a lunar cycle, and is 29–30 days long. Because of this, the Muslim year is a few days shorter than a Western year, and Muslim festivals, although they fall on the same day in the Muslim calendar, fall on different dates in the Western calendar.

These are the dates of the most important Muslim festivals.

1 Muharram: the Day of Hijra (the Muslim New Year, which remembers Muhammad's (pbuh) journey from Makkah to **Madinah**)

10 Safar: Ashura

12 Rabi ul-Awwal: Maulid ul-Nabi (Muhammad's (pbuh) birthday)

27 Rajab: Isra' wal Mir'aj (Muhammad's (pbuh) night journey, when he was taken to heaven)

27 Ramadan: Lailat-ul-Qadr (the Night of Power, when Muhammad (pbuh) began to receive the Qur'an)

1 Shawwal: Id-ul-Fitr (celebrates the end of the month of fasting)

10 Dhul Hijja: Id-ul-Adha (remembers the story of Ibrahim (pbuh) and Isma'il (pbuh))

Pilgrimage – Hajj 1

In this section you will:

● read about the reasons for making pilgrimage to Makkah

● understand the nature and importance of entering the state of ihram

● develop an awareness of the spiritual transformation that Hajj can have in the lives of Muslim pilgrims.

Pilgrimage to Makkah

Hajj is the fifth pillar of **Islam**. It is a pilgrimage to **Makkah** and is to be made at least once in a lifetime by those **Muslims** who can afford to do so.

When Muslims pray they face the direction of Makkah. In fact they face the **Ka'bah**, the House of Allah, which Muslims believe was built originally by **Adam** (the first man) and later rebuilt by the prophet **Ibrahim** and his son **Isma'il** (peace be upon them all). It was the first house ever built for the sole purpose of the worship of Allah. Muslims believe that Allah has blessed the Ka'bah. Every year, Muslims who can afford to make the journey and are physically fit come here from all over the world to join fellow Muslims in worship in Allah's House.

During Hajj the Islamic community (the **ummah**) becomes particularly evident and can be experienced in a special way by everyone who takes part. Barriers of language, territory, colour and race disappear as the bond of **faith** is strengthened. Everyone has the same status in the House of Allah – the status of His servant.

The Ka'bah

'It was the most amazing moment of my life. Standing before God at the foot of Mount Mercy with 2,000,000 of my fellow Muslims really did bring my faith alive for me. I have always tried hard to keep the teachings of the Qur'an, and live my life as a good person, but this was different. Everything that I have ever been taught, the events in the life of the Prophet that I had only heard about was real. To bear witness with so many others is an experience that I shall never forget.'

Mamood, aged 24 – **Hajji**

Muslims in ihram

Ihram

While approaching Makkah before the Hajj begins, a pilgrim must put on ihram. For men, ihram consists of two sheets of unsewn white cloth. This is a very simple form of dress which male pilgrims must wear in place of their normal everyday clothes. For a woman, ihram does not require special clothes, but they do have to dress simply and wear a veil covering their hair.

This change is very significant. It reminds the pilgrim of his position in relation to Allah. He is a humble servant of his Creator. It also reminds him that after death he will be wrapped in white sheets; not in expensive or fashionable clothes.

There are restrictions on pilgrims while in the state of ihram. He or she must not:

● use perfume

● kill or harm animals, even insects

● break or uproot plants

● do anything dishonest or arrogant

● carry weapons

● cover the head (males)

● cover the face (females)

● wear shoes covering ankles

● cut hair

● clip nails

● have sexual relations.

United before Allah

Hajj brings together Muslims from all around the world. It also brings together Muslims from the two main groups within Islam – Sunni Muslims and Shi'ah Muslims.

Following the death of Muhammad (pbuh) there were disagreements as to who should lead the Muslims. Those who supported the **prophet's** descendants as leaders became known as the 'Shiat Ali' or the Party of Ali. They are now called Shi'ites. They do not accept the first three **khalifahs** who ruled Islam following the death of Muhammad (pbuh). They claimed that Ali was really the first true leader after Muhammad (pbuh), followed by the prophet's grandsons Hasan and Husayn.

Sunnah is the Arabic word for 'custom' or 'authority'. Sunni Muslims regard themselves as the true followers of the Sunnah, or the example of the prophet Muhammad (pbuh). They insist that Muhammad (pbuh) had intended elections so that the best man would succeed as leader, and not to start a family line of rulers.

Ninety per cent of all Muslims are Sunnis. The Shi'ites, on the other hand, make up only 10 per cent of modern Muslims.

Pilgrimage – Hajj 2

In this section you will:

- find out about the duties performed by Muslims on Hajj
- reflect upon the importance of each duty of Hajj
- learn about the story of Ibrahim (pbuh) and Isma'il (pbuh) in the Qur'an.

The duties of Hajj

Muslims performing **Hajj** and in a state of ihram can truly be described as one equal family before **Allah**. It is as one family that the essential duties or rituals of Hajj are performed.

- The **Ka'bah** is circled seven times. The Ka'bah is thought by Muslims to be the very first place used to worship Allah. Pilgrims run between the hills of **Safa** and **Marwah** where **Hajar**, wife of the prophet **Ibrahim** (**pbuh**), desperately searched for water for her child.

Allah provided water in the form of the Well of Zamzam where pilgrims still stop to drink and to fill bottles to take some of the water home.

- Pilgrims then travel out of Makkah along the plain of **Arafat**. Here around two million pilgrims camp as they perform the next duties of Hajj.

- Pilgrims stand together before Allah on Mount Arafat (The Mount of Mercy). It is an opportunity to commit oneself again to Allah and to follow His laws in all aspects of life.

- The camp then moves on to Muzdalifah, which is between Arafat and Makkah. Here pilgrims collect small stones to throw at the pillars at **Mina**.

- Mina is the where the prophet Ibrahim (pbuh) and his family resisted the temptations of the devil to turn away from Allah and to put their trust in him. Pilgrims throw stones at three stone pillars that represent the devil. This symbolizes a rejection of both the devil that tempted Ibrahim (pbuh) and also at the 'devil' inside that leads everyone into temptation.

1 The Great Mosque 3 Mina 5 Plain of Arafat
2 The Ka'bah 4 Muzdalifah 6 The Mount of Mercy

The route of the Hajj

- The pilgrims then camp at Mina for two days to celebrate the Feast of Sacrifice (**Id-ul-Adha**). An animal is sacrificed in thanksgiving for the ram Allah gave Ibrahim (pbuh), just as Ibrahim (pbuh) was about to sacrifice his son **Isma'il** (pbuh) to Allah.

- As an outward sign of the completion of the duties of Hajj men will have their heads shaved (unfurling) and women at least 2.5cm cut from their hair.

- Pilgrims will then return to Makkah to circle the Ka'bah again before returning to their homes.

Male Muslims who have performed Hajj are entitled to take the name **Hajji** and women **Hajjah**.

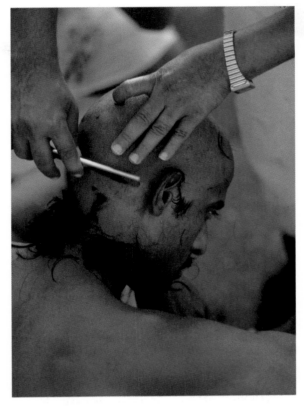

The unfurling

Id-ul-Adha

Id-ul-Adha remembers the story of Ibrahim (pbuh) told in the **Qur'an** – a story of unwavering **faith** and submission to Allah's will.

Ibrahim (pbuh) had made a promise to dedicate his life to the will of Allah. One night Ibrahim (pbuh) had a dream in which he was asked to sacrifice his only son Isma'il (pbuh) to Allah. He was distraught, but he spoke to his son and they agreed to do what Ibrahim (pbuh) had been commanded to do.

They travelled to Mina, where the sacrifice was to take place. Isma'il (pbuh) lay face down on the altar, ready to be sacrificed. At the last moment, however, Allah stopped Ibrahim (pbuh) and gave him a ram to sacrifice in place of his son.

Rules for pilgrims

Muslims who perform Hajj must first fulfil certain criteria. First of all, they must be Muslims – non-Muslims are not permitted to take part in the pilgrimage. They must be physically fit and mentally sound, so that they can cope with and fully understand the purpose of their actions. They must also have enough funds both to pay for their pilgrimage by honest means, and to support any dependants they leave behind during Hajj.

Rites of passage

In this section you will:

- discover the ways in which Muslims celebrate birth
- understand the importance of marriage in the Muslim community
- learn about the customs of the naming ceremony for babies and the importance of choosing the baby's name.

Everyone enjoys a celebration. Finding an excuse for a party or sharing a good time with family and friends is not difficult. However, the reasons behind some celebrations are very important – the birth of a baby or the joining together of two people in marriage are important to both religious and non-religious people alike. This is an opportunity to discover something of the way in which **Muslims** mark these two special occasions, referred to as rites of passage, in a special way.

Birth

For Muslims, the birth of a baby is a reason for great joy. Muslims believe that **Allah** has granted the family the blessing of a son or daughter and so should receive their thanks and praise.

A new born baby hearing the adhan for the first time

The new baby is welcomed into the community of **Islam** as soon as it is born, as the head of the family whispers the **adhan** (the call to prayer) into its ear. Therefore, the first word the baby hears is 'Allah'. Prayers, usually led by the community's imam, are said for the baby and the family.

Marriage

Muhammad (**pbuh**) said:

'A woman should only be married to a person who is good enough for her or compatible to her.'

Hadith

For Muslims, the only sort of compatibility that really matters is **faith**. Muhammad (pbuh) permitted marriages between people of vastly different social status and financial backgrounds, knowing that compatibility depended more on what they were like in their hearts and in their devotion to Allah.

The most important ingredients in a Muslim marriage are shared values and **beliefs**, so that even if the couple come from different cultures and backgrounds, they will possess the same basic religious attitudes and practices which will help to bind them ever closer together.

'Do not marry only for a person's looks, their beauty might become the cause of moral decline.'

'Do not marry for wealth, since this may become the cause of disobedience. Marry rather on the grounds of religious devotion.'

Hadiths

Islam regards marriage as the normal duty of every human being. Finding a good life partner, and building up a relationship together is regarded as an essential part of the faith.

A Muslim marriage

The Muslim marriage service is a social ceremony rather than a religious one and so can take place anywhere licensed for marriages. However, prayers seeking Allah's blessing led by the imam, will be said for the couple and their families.

In the Muslim world, there is often little contact between young men and women. The selection of a marriage partner is often made by the parents. Sometimes they will look for a known member of the family, preferably a cousin. For many couples, love is expected to come after the marriage and not before.

It is true to say that today, in some Muslim families, customs are changing a little with regards to the selection of marriage partners. Although there is still an expectation that partners will be suitable for each other in the eyes of their families, some couples are happier considering for themselves their own suitability for each other.

'The best of treasures is a good wife. She is pleasing in her husband's eyes, looks for ways to please him, and takes care of his possessions while he is away, the best of you are those who treat their wives best.'

Hadith

Muslim names

Seven days after the birth of a Muslim baby comes the celebration of aqiqah. This is when relatives and friends come to a feast and the baby is named.

First of all, the baby's head is shaved, and by tradition gold or silver of the same weight as the hair is given to the poor. Even if the baby has no hair, a donation of money is still given. Some Muslims also offer a sacrifice, a sheep or a goat for a feast with friends, to give thanks for the birth.

The choice of name is important. In fact, choosing the name is seen as one of the most important duties a parent can carry out. The chosen name is usually a family name or one of the names from **Muhammad's (pbuh)** family.

For boys, some of the names often chosen start with '**Abd**', which means 'slave'. Abd will be added to one of the 99 different names for Allah, for example, Abdullah (Servant of God), Abdul Rahman (Slave of the Merciful) and Abdul Karim (Slave of the Generous One). This shows that whatever else they may do or become in life, it the first duty of every Muslim to be a faithful servant of Allah.

Khitan

All Muslim baby boys are circumcised. This involves cutting the foreskin from the penis. Circumcision is the ancient practice of the prophets and is seen as a special sign to show that one belongs to Allah. Circumcision is not regarded as cruel. It is in fact seen by some as a healthy practice, especially in some of the hottest countries of the world.

Creation

In this section you will:

- find out about Muslim beliefs regarding the creation of the universe
- gain an understanding about Muslim food laws and halal and haram foods
- read about which foods are prohibited (haram) for Muslims.

Earth from space

The power of Allah

Most religious traditions have developed an account of **creation** that depicts the central involvement of God. The **Qur'an** is very clear as to the origins of all things, all things derive their being from **Allah** and to Allah shall all return when their time on earth is over.

'It is Allah who has created the heavens and the earth, and all that is between them in six days. Then he rose to His throne that suits His majesty. Mankind has no God besides Allah, as protector and helper. Remember this, Allah manages and regulates every thing on earth and in heaven and when every thing has had its time it will return to Him.'

'Allah alone is the all-knower of the seen and unseen, the all-mighty, the most merciful. It was He who created all goodness and began the creation of Mankind from clay. Then He made offspring – male and female. Then He made all other living things upon earth.'

Qur'an, from surahs 21 and 32

At the completion of His creation Allah declared:

'Have they not looked at the heaven above them, how We have made it and adorned it, and there are no rifts in it?

And the earth! We have spread it out, and set thereon mountains standing firm, and have produced therein every kind of lovely growth in pairs.'

Qur'an, **surah** 50: 6–7

The creation

Muslims have a very clear understanding of how the whole universe came about: it was created by Allah. The Qur'an teaches that all things were summoned into existence at Allah's command in pairs so that creation may be seen as a perfectly balanced order. Such a balance can be understood in the creation of the sky and the earth, the sea and dry land, light and darkness and male and female.

In common with the Jewish Torah and Christian Bible the Qur'an tells of creation covering six days. However, Muslims are certain that if Allah had wished, He could have created everything in just 'a twinkling of the eye'.

Similarly, the Qur'an mentions the creation of beings for whom creation is not mentioned in either the Torah or Bible.

For example, Muslims believe in common with Jews and Christians that human beings were created from clay, they also believe that **angels** (slaves of Allah who always do His will) were created from light and that **jinn** (beings created with free will, living on earth in a separate yet parallel world to our own) were created from fire. However, of all of Allah's creations, this planet and in particular the human beings that inhabit it are the most important.

A famous story illustrates the importance of the creation of humans. After the creation of **Adam** (**pbuh**), the first man, Allah brought all the angels and all the jinn before Adam (pbuh) and commanded them to bow down to him as he was the most wonderful thing that Allah had ever created. All the angels and jinn bowed down with the exception of one jinn called **Shaytan** (the Devil). As a punishment Allah banished Shaytan from His presence and in return Shaytan vowed to spend all his time and power tempting humans to go against the will of Allah and to sin.

Haram foods

Haram (prohibited) foods include:

- any products made from a pig
- meat containing blood
- meat from an animal which dies due to disease or other natural causes
- any flesh-eating animal
- any animal that has been killed either by another animal or by any means made haram by Allah
- any animal that has been sacrificed to idols.

Food laws

Like many other religions, **Islam** teaches that some foods are allowed (**halal**) and some foods are forbidden (haram).

Muslims are allowed to eat all types of fruit, vegetables and grains. The main restrictions are related to animal products. In order to be halal, an animal which is killed has to have all the blood in it drained away. Islamic law requires the animal to be killed by a sharp knife in the neck, which allows this to happen. Allah's name is repeated over the animal to show that the food is being taken with God's permission.

Meat of animals not slain in this way is regarded as haram. Even the marrow, rennet and gelatine of these animals are haram. Efforts should be made to obtain halal meat from Muslim butchers, and Muslims have to take care that they do not eat haram food 'hidden' in other products.

Environment

In this section you will:

● understand the Muslim belief that all creation is Allah's

● read about the ways in which Muslims care for animals and the earth

● find out about the Muslim contribution to the Assisi Declaration 1986.

Allah's gift of creation

Muslims believe that **Allah** has given this planet to humankind to look after and protect. The **Qur'an** teaches that human beings have been created by Allah and placed on earth to act as stewards (**khalifah**) and take responsibility for every part of Allah's creation. They are expected not to pollute or damage the world. Instead they are expected to protect the fine balance that makes up Allah's creation. As a result, Muslims are commanded to make careful use of resources like water, respect animals and replace natural resources used wherever possible.

'It is He who has made you custodians, inheritors of the Earth.'

Qur'an, **surah** 6: 165

Care for all creatures

Muslims can expect to be judged by Allah on their stewardship of His creation, including all creatures and all the natural resources which He has given.

Many Muslims are concerned with the well being of the other creatures, besides human beings that Allah has placed on the planet. It is true that some animals have been given by Allah as food but **Muhammad (pbuh)** banned any 'sport' which involved making animals fight each other, which was common in his time. Therefore, modern blood sports such as fox-hunting are condemned by Islam.

Islam teaches that no one should ever hunt just for amusement. Muslims believe that people should only take the life of animals for food or another useful purpose.

A tropical rain forest

Respecting all that Allah has created

'If someone kills a sparrow for sport, the sparrow will cry out on the Day of Judgement, "O Lord! That person killed me for nothing! He did not kill me for any useful purpose!"'

Hadith

All hunting should be for food, and any animal used for hunting should be well trained and kept under control.

Experiments are carried out on animals for a variety of reasons. Some of these are medical others are for cosmetic purposes. According to the principle of compassion and kindness towards all Allah's creations, any experiment simply for the development of luxury goods is forbidden. Muslims should always find out if the things they buy have been produced using **halal** (permitted by Allah) methods.

With regard to medical experiments, if there were no possible alternative to an experiment on an animal, then Muslims might accept it. However, they would prefer to look for some other method of investigation.

'Allah it is He who has subjected … to you all that is in the Heavens and all that is in the Earth.'

Qur'an, surah 45: 12–13

Human responsibility

Muslims believe that Allah has given people free will and it is as free agents that we decide how we treat the planet we live on. However, Islam teaches that this planet is a place created out of love, and therefore it should be looked after through love.

Islam teaches that Muslims should seek to live at peace with nature, and to bring about a oneness between human beings and the rest of Allah's creation.

The Assisi Declaration 1986

In 1986 Muslims were among the representatives of all the major world religions meeting in Assisi. They met to discuss the role they intended to play, as people of faith, in the world. Most importantly, they explored their role in looking after the world for the use and enjoyment of future generations.

The place and timing of the meeting was no accident. Assisi was the home of a man called St Francis. Although a Christian, he has been accepted by many people of different faiths as someone who had a particular love for nature and cared for it deeply.

1986 marked the 25th anniversary of the World Wide Fund for Nature, an organization set up to work on behalf of the earth's natural environment in the face of ever-expanding world industrialization.

All the different faiths made statements regarding 'religion and nature'. Muslims declared: 'Allah's trustees are responsible for maintaining the unity of His creation, its flora, its fauna, its wildlife and natural environment … Unity cannot be had by setting one need against another or one end over another; it is maintained by balance and harmony.'

Abuses of Allah's creation

In this section you will:

● develop an understanding of creation as Allah's gift to humanity

● consider ways in which people abuse Allah's gift

● reflect upon living in a multicultural society and the importance of living with respect.

The **Qur'an** teaches that we have been placed on earth to act as stewards (**khalifah**). This means to look after **Allah**'s creation on His behalf. Sadly, there is a good deal of evidence to suggest that we do not always do a very satisfactory job. Many people abuse Allah's created order by a misuse of nature and worse still by abusing the greatest of all Allah's creation, themselves.

The planet

Abuse of Allah's creation goes on all around the world. One of the main concerns is the ways in which the vast tropical rain forests are being cut down at a very fast rate. It may well be the case that the timber cut is required for building projects, or the land cleared needed to graze herds of cattle, but the rain forests have been provided by Allah for a particular reason. Carbon dioxide, produced when something is burned, is turned into oxygen by trees. The more trees the more oxygen, but fewer trees means more carbon dioxide in the atmosphere.

Ourselves

Another concern held by **Muslims** is the way in which people abuse themselves by the use of alcohol. The use of all alcohol is strictly

Destroying the rain forest

Muhammad spoke out against the use of alcohol

forbidden in **Islam**. This applies not only to wine which existed at the time of **Muhammad** (**pbuh**) but also to any other form of alcohol. The main reason for this is that alcohol can cause people to lose control over their own minds and bodies. A famous story told by Muslims illustrates this fact well.

'Intoxicants are the key to all evils. A man was brought and asked either to tear the Holy Qur'an, or kill a child, or bow in worship to an idol, or drink alcohol, or sleep with a woman. He thought the less sinful thing was to drink the alcohol, so he drank it. Then he slept with the woman, killed the child, tore the Holy Qur'an and bowed in worship of the idol.'

A Muslim tale

Islam teaches that **Shaytan** uses different ways to turn people away from belief in Allah, and alcohol is just one.

At the time of Muhammad (pbuh), many people enjoyed drinking alcohol. The teaching of Allah in the Qur'an took human weakness into account, and the prohibition of alcohol was given in stages.

As the news of this latest revelation spread through Madinah, the city in which Muhammad (pbuh) was living, the effect was amazing. People poured away the drinks they held in their hands, and smashed their wine containers, pouring the liquid away. Few, if any, true Muslims have ever touched alcohol since.

Living with respect

We as human beings are but a small part of Allah's universe. However, we are a very important part because Allah has granted us stewardship of his creation.

Many people would want to suggest that the best way to look after the country in which we live is to begin by treating all those that live in our society with respect. Only by working together can we treat our environment with respect.

Britain is a multicultural society. This means that people from a wide variety of religious, national and ethnic backgrounds live in Britain today. One hundred years ago it may have easily been assumed that your neighbours would have been white, British-born and claim to be Christian. Today this is not the case. In 1991, in the last census for which figures are available (the 2001 census is still being analysed), 5.5 per cent of the population was made up of ethnic groups other than white British. This was more than 3 million people, and this figure has certainly increased since then. Living together with mutual respect is a positive way to look after Allah's creation.

'Prejudice' means to pre-judge someone or a group of people, usually in a bad way. 'Discrimination' means to act unfairly towards someone or a group of people, based on pre-judged ideas.

Both prejudice and discrimination are wrong and must be overcome.

Human rights

In this section you will:
- discover what is meant by 'human rights'
- understand the importance of basic human rights for Muslims.

Human rights and responsibilities

Islam teaches that all human beings have been created by **Allah**. As a result **Muslims** believe that there are basic rights which are shared by all people and which should be observed in every society, whether the society is Islamic or not.

These human rights have been granted by Allah, and not by any ruler or government, and it is the duty of Muslims to protect them actively. Failure to do so can lead to people being oppressed and living life in misery. Muslims believe that human life is sacred, and that all human beings should be treated with respect.

The earth has many wonderful resources, and there is enough for everyone to live well. No human being should know hunger while others are able to waste what they have. Islam teaches that the needs of the suffering must be met. The hungry should be fed, the naked clothed, and the wounded or diseased given medical treatment, whether they are Muslim or not, and whether they are friends or enemies.

The ummah before Allah

Sufferers of famine

Muslims also believe that the honour and dignity of every individual is important. Therefore, ridicule is never seen as fun, especially when there is arrogance or malice behind it. Muslims believe that we may laugh with people, to share in the happiness of life but we must never laugh at people which may cause them distress or embarrassment.

Muslims believe that no attempt should ever be made to force people to act against their own will, so long as they are not acting against the best interests of others.

Muslims believe that no human being should ever be imprisoned unless they are proved guilty of some crime, in an open and unbiased court.

Muslims believe that the power of any human being is only given on trust from Allah. It is therefore their duty to speak out against dictators, and protect the weak from those who would oppress them. To Muslims, a dictator is a ruler who attempts to assert his own will upon the people, rather than seek for them the will of Allah which is always based on kindness and justice.

Protecting people's freedom

It is the duty of an Islamic state to promote right and forbid wrong (**Qur'an**, **surah** 22: 44).

According to the Qur'an, the state is responsible for the welfare of all its citizens – Muslims and non-Muslims alike. It should grant the basic necessities of life. All citizens of an Islamic state should enjoy freedom of **belief**, thought, conscience and speech. Every citizen should be free to develop their potential and earn a living wage. All citizens should enjoy the right to speak out on issues they consider right or wrong, remembering that the Islamic state is duty bound to implement the laws of the Qur'an.

Some Muslims are disappointed that there is not a single perfect Islamic state in the world today. It is true that there are many Muslim countries. Many feel that a true Islamic state should be based on the model of prophet **Muhammad's** (**pbuh**) state in **Madinah**.

However, organized efforts are being made in many parts of the world to bring about total change in society by setting up an Islamic system of government to fully implement the laws of the Qur'an. It is hoped that Islamic states will emerge from these efforts which will guide the problem-torn world towards justice, happiness and peace.

Caring for others – Zakah

In this section you will:

● investigate zakah, the third pillar of Islam

● reflect upon ways in which zakah can make a difference in the lives of all Muslims

● learn about Muslim laws regarding earning and spending money.

A Muslim making a zakah contribution

Caring for others

All **Muslims** are expected to be charitable in hospitality and in caring for the wider community. For example a baker's shop could give away what it had left on a Thursday night, so that no one nearby need say their Friday prayers hungry. Similarly, a Muslim could send money to support an appeal or disaster fund.

The **prophet Muhammad** (**pbuh**) encouraged giving:

'He who eats and drinks while his brother goes hungry, is not one of us.'

Hadith

'Every day two **angels** come down from Heaven; one of them says "O **Allah**! Compensate every person who gives in Your name.' The other says "O Allah! Destroy every miser!"'

Hadith

Zakah

In addition to such charitable giving, Muslims are expected to share their income and wealth as a matter of duty, and to hand over a certain proportion each year to support those who are less fortunate in the community. This is not

regarded as a matter of choice, but as a religious duty and is called **zakah**.

Zakah is the third pillar of **Islam**. The Arabic word 'zakah' means 'to purify or cleanse'. Zakah is to be paid once a year on savings at the rate of two-and-a-half percent. Payment of zakah is a means of keeping wealth clear of greed and selfishness. It also encourages Muslims to be honest.

Zakah is a compulsory payment and is not seen by Muslims as a charity or a tax. Charity is optional and taxes can be used by the state for any purpose, but zakah has to be spent for purposes like helping the poor, the needy,

Helping the poor

Rates of zakah

Wealth	Amount	Rate
Cash in hand or bank	Over the value of 595g of silver	2.5%
Gold and silver	85g of gold or 595g of silver	2.5%
Trading goods	To the value of 595g of silver	2.5%
Cows	30	1
Goats and sheep	40	1
Mining produce	Any	20%
Agricultural produce	Per harvest: Rain watered land Irrigated	10% 5%

payment of salaries to its collectors, to free captives and debtors, and for travellers in need. Zakah is an act of worship and obedience. Muslims pay zakah to gain Allah's favour. Zakah provides Muslims with the opportunity of sharing wealth with those less fortunate.

Muslims see wealth as really belonging to Allah. He is seen as the real owner and people are merely the trustees of His wealth. Through the payment of zakah, the rich share their wealth with the poor and thus a fair distribution of resources is ensured.

A duty of care

Islam is a way of life. More than just a group of believers, Muslims have a duty of care for each other in the name of Allah. The way in which Muslims approach the acquisition and distribution of wealth reflects this point well.

Muslims appreciate that economics are complex, but they argue that the effort should be made to ensure a fairer distribution of wealth and resources around both the national and world economies.

The Muslim economic system

Islamic laws govern the ways in which Muslims can earn and spend their money. In addition to the duty to make zakah contributions, Muslims may not:

● earn money from the production or sale of alcoholic drinks, from gambling and lotteries

● earn money by illegal means, such as theft, deceit, fraud and so on

● earn money through any transactions which involve charging interest, which Islam teaches is a means of exploitation.

Muslims see the approach of the modern 'free market economy' as against the most basic of Allah's wishes for humankind – that fairness and justice should be available to all. Islam teaches that a system of zakah distributes wealth more fairly (rich to poor) than a system like a free market which is, it is said, designed to redistribute resources from poor to rich.

Women in Islam

In this section you will:

● find out about what the Qur'an teaches regarding the status of women in Islam

● think about issues relating to modern Muslim women

● read and reflect upon words from the Qur'an regarding women.

Women have a very important place in **Islamic** society. The importance of women as mothers and as wives was made clear by **Muhammad (pbuh)**:

'Paradise lies at the feet of your mothers.'

Once a person asked Muhammad (pbuh), 'Who deserves the best care from me?' The prophet replied, 'Your mother, then your mother then your mother then your father and then your nearest relatives.'

'O people, your wives have certain rights over you and you have certain rights over them.'

The prophet also said:

'The best amongst you is the one who is best towards his wife.'

Hadiths

These sayings indicate the important position that should be granted to women in Islam. However, there are some people who have misgivings about the status of women in Islam. For some, a **Muslim** woman is seen almost as a prisoner in the four walls of her own house, a non-person, someone who has no rights and is living under the domination of men.

A group of Muslim women

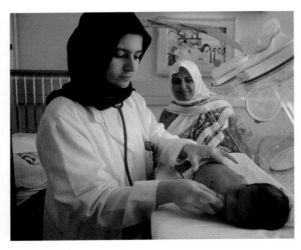

A Muslim woman at work

Muslims believe that **Allah** has created all living creatures in pairs, male and female, including humankind. Allah has honoured the children of **Adam** (pbuh) both male and female. As a result, Muslim women have certain rights and responsibilities, for example, the right to choose their husband. No one can impose a decision on a woman against her will. She has a right to seek separation from her husband if their marriage becomes impossible to sustain.

A woman has a right to develop her talents and to work. Islam allows a non-Muslim married woman to keep and practise her religion and her husband cannot interfere with this freedom. This would apply for example to Christian and Jewish women with Muslim husbands.

It is the duty of the Muslim mother to bring up children according to the **faith** of Islam, to look after the family and control domestic affairs. Muslim women should dress modestly, as should Muslim men. In some Muslim countries, Women put on **hijab** (a covering cloak) while going out and meeting adult males other than close relatives.

Islam views a husband and wife as complementary to each other. Neither should dominate the other. Each has his or her own individual rights and duties and together they should form a peaceful and happy family, which Islam teaches is the basis for a sound and prosperous society.

Women and Allah

The significance of Muslim women as an important half of the human race, created and loved by Allah, is clear in this passage from the Qur'an.

'The Muslims, men and women,
the believers, men and women,
the men and women who are obedient,
the men and women who are truthful,
the men and women who are patient,
the men and women who are humble,
the men and women who give *sadaqah*
    (**zakah** and alms to the poor),
the men and women who observe **sawm**
    (fasting during **Ramadan**),
the men and women who guard their
    chastity
and the men and women who remember
    Allah much with their hearts and
    tongues,
Allah has prepared for them forgiveness
    and a great reward (Paradise).'

One of the teachings of Islam is that men and women, although different, are created equal as spiritual beings before Allah. All the teachings of Islam given in the Qur'an speak to both male and female Muslims.

On one occasion, the wife of Muhammad (pbuh) spoke to him about this. Allah provided Muhammad (pbuh) with a special message to explain that the term 'man' in the Qur'an's revelations referred to 'all human beings' and not just male human beings.

All people, male and female, are expected to follow the religion that Allah has presented to them, and they will be judged together according to their faithfulness.

Matters of life and death

In this section you will:

● understand what is meant by the term 'human life is sacred'

● consider Islamic teaching regarding the afterlife

● reflect upon Islamic teaching about issues surrounding abortion.

Muslims believe that all human life is a gift of **Allah**, and is therefore sacred.

'Do not kill anyone … killing Allah has forbidden.'
Qur'an, surah 17: 33

'It is He, Allah, Who makes laugh, and makes weep. It is Allah Who causes death and gives life. And that He Allah creates the pairs, male and female.'

Qur'an, surah 53: 42–5

Muslims believe that Allah has given every life an allotted span. No human being knows when their life will be required by Allah and taken back. Therefore, it is the duty of all Muslims to live every day as if it was their last in readiness for the moment when they will face Allah and answer to Him for what they have done with their lives.

'The knowledge of the Final Hour is with Allah; none can reveal the time but He. It shall not come upon you except all of a sudden.'

Qur'an, surah 7: 187

Islam teaches that death itself should never be feared. It is human nature to dread pain and suffering, but Muslims should do their best to bear everything with patience and fortitude. Death is the natural end of human life. It cannot be avoided, and no one escapes it.

'When their time comes, neither can they delay nor can they advance it an hour.'

Qur'an, surah 16: 61

Muslims should not fear death, nor consider it to be the end of everything, as they believe in the promise of an afterlife. This should be a time of great joy and reward for all their efforts on earth.

In effect human life is one eternal life made up of two parts, life before and life after death. Muslims believe that the spirit of life that Allah has breathed into everyone is raised by Allah, from death to the afterlife.

'Do you think that We shall not reassemble your bones? Yes, We are able to put together in perfect order the tips of fingers!'

Qur'an, surah 75: 3

Islam, therefore, teaches that death is beyond human control. No person can choose the time of their passing – it is Allah alone who sanctions the hour of death.

'No person can die except by Allah's leave and after an appointed term.'

Qur'an, surah 3: 145

A Muslim tombstone

Islam teaches that funerals should not be expensive. Muslims prefer that coffins should not be used, except to comply with local regulations for health reasons. Ideally, the body should be buried simply in the earth, and should be carried to the cemetery.

Muslims are usually buried with their face turned to the right, facing **Makkah**. It is therefore preferable if they can have their own cemeteries, or their own special plot so that they may have their graves facing in the right direction.

As the body is lowered, they say:

'In the name of God we commit you to the earth, according to the Way of the **Prophet** of God.'

A little earth is then thrown down with the words:

'We created you from it, and We return you into it, and from it We will raise you a second time.'

Qur'an, surah 20: 55

Money should not be spent on elaborate tombstones or memorials, but donations given to the poor.

Mourning should not last for more than three days, except for widows who may mourn for four months and ten days, and should not remarry during that period.

Last words

When death is very near for a Muslim, it is important for the person to be surrounded by family and friends. The person will ask their forgiveness and Allah's forgiveness for any wrongdoing. If possible, the last words they say will be the **shahadah**, the declaration of **faith** in Allah.

Moral dilemmas

Muslims believe that human life is sacred. However, should this make a difference to the way in which they think about other people?

The situations below are examples of moral dilemmas of the type that may face Muslims in Britain today, and the way in which they might respond to them.

❶ An unmarried woman falls pregnant and is uncertain about how she feels. She is faced with a number of possibilities:

- to have the baby and bring it up
- to have the baby and put it up for adoption
- to have an abortion (an operation to end the pregnancy and remove the baby from the womb).

Islam teaches that all life is a gift from Allah and, as such, should be respected. Therefore, it appears at first that Muslims would be totally against abortion. However, Islam teaches that the spirit which gives a person their unique personality does not develop until the fourth month of pregnancy. This would indicate that, although not the ideal, an abortion would be permissible in certain circumstances.

❷ A 63-year-old grandfather is diagnosed as suffering from an incurable form of cancer. He has been told that he will die soon and will suffer a lot of pain. He asks a doctor to end his life painlessly with a lethal injection before the cancer takes a complete hold on his body. The request is denied.

53

Jihad

In this section you will:

● investigate the nature of jihad in Islam

● explore the reasons for the inclusion of jihad in the Muslim life of faith

● read and reflect upon prayers for peace from three different religions.

The nature of jihad

Jihad is an Arabic word that means 'striving'. **Muslims** use the word jihad to refer to any activity undertaken for the love of **Allah**. Jihad is the use of all one's energies and resources to establish the **Islamic** way of life. Jihad is, therefore, a continuous process for Muslims.

'The aim of jihad is to establish peace. At first we learn to control bad desires and intentions. Human beings must strive hard to achieve this. This is jihad within ourselves and is the basis for the jihad which is concerned with establishing right and removing evil from lives and from society, to establish peace.'

Imam Aurangzeb Khan

Therefore, jihad demands the use of all material and mental resources. It may be the case that Muslims may be required to give their lives for the cause of Islam.

The aim of jihad is to seek the pleasure of Allah. This must not be forgotten because this purpose is the basis of all Islamic practice. Jihad fits alongside the basic duties of **shahadah**, **salah**, **zakah**, **sawm** and **Hajj**. All these duties teach obedience to Allah and seek His favour so that Muslims may reap the reward of entering Paradise, the place of joy and peace, when they die.

Muslim soldiers

All Islamic duties should prepare Muslims to engage in jihad. Jihad is at the heart of faith and the end result of salah, zakah, sawm and Hajj.

'It is most important that we try hard to practise what we say.'

Imam Aurangzeb Khan

'Why do you ask of others the right conduct and you yourselves forget, have you no sense?'

Qur'an, surah 2: 44

The importance of jihad

'O you who believe! Why do you say that which you do not do? It is most hateful to Allah that you say that which you do not.'

Qur'an, surah 61: 2–3

These verses clearly direct Muslims to put words into action. To achieve this, Muslims carry out their duty to do good themselves and urge others to do the same. This can, and often does, include getting involved in charity and relief organizations like the Red Crescent (the Islamic version of the Red Cross).

However, jihad can also result in a violent struggle in order to establish the Islamic way of life. Such an outcome is tragic as Islam teaches that violence is prohibited unless absolutely necessary. Wherever possible, jihad is centred around changing hearts and minds by peaceful persuasion rather than by force.

A Red Crescent refugee camp

Prayers for peace

All of the major world religions teach that at the heart of God is peace. Therefore, they all have prayers for peace in a world torn apart by war. Here are three examples:

Lord, make us instruments of your peace.
Where there is hatred, let us sow love,
Where there is injury, pardon,
Where there is doubt, faith,
Where there is despair, hope,
Where there is sadness, joy.

(Christianity)

Oh Allah, you are peace.
You are the source of peace.
You are full of blessings and sublime.

(Islam)

Cause us, our Father, to lie down in peace,
And rise again to enjoy life.
Spread over us the covering of your peace,
Guide us with your good counsel
And save us for the sake of your name.

(Judaism)

Evil and suffering

In this section you will:

● think about what is meant by the problem of evil

● consider Muslim responses to the claim that blame for evil and suffering in the world should be laid before Allah

● read about how a young Muslim gained an understanding of Allah's will.

Everyday the media brings us headlines about things many would describe as 'evil', or about great 'suffering'.

Young family dies in house fire

Man convicted of murder

Earthquake kills thousands

Famine threatens Ethiopia

Leukaemia sufferer, 14, emergency bone marrow transplant essential

The effects of an earthquake

The problem of evil and suffering

Everyday people ask the question 'why?' Why, if there is an almighty God who has created all things out of love and compassion are we to suffer? Is it not impossible to believe in something all-powerful and all-loving that allows evil and suffering to exist? It would seem that either God is not all-powerful or else not all-loving, as evil and suffering clearly exist.

'I look at the sun, moon, sky, lakes and wonderful things like that that Allah can do. Then I look beyond these things, the wonderful things, and I see flooding, hurricanes and droughts. I ask myself, "How can Allah allow such things?"'

Anish, aged 13

Muslim responses

Muslims believe that **Allah** is indeed all-powerful and all-loving and for that reason has granted to all created things free will. It is the murderer who freely decides to take a life and the free and natural course of things for earthquakes to occur.

Muslims believe that the will of Allah is beyond human understanding and therefore impossible to rationalize. Muslims in their prayers will often add 'If Allah wills' as they know that all things beyond our control are in Allah's hands and that they should trust His judgement.

'Or do you think that you shall enter Paradise without such trials as came to those who passed away before you?'

Qur'an, surah 2: 214

'Revile not destiny, for, behold, I am Destiny.'

Hadith

A personal reflection

There was once a young Muslim called Salim. One day when he was 13 years old he returned home from school and was met by his father, who told him some very sad news. Salim's father explained that his mother was suffering from cancer. It was expected that she would not live for more than 5 or 6 months.

Salim was a tense mixture of many emotions. He felt deep, deep sorrow. He felt helpless, and he even felt guilty. Most of all he felt angry – angry that Allah, a God of love and compassion, could allow such a thing to happen to his wonderful mother who, at 35, was far too young to die.

He prayed. He prayed for what seemed like hours every day telling Allah exactly how he felt. He was angry. Salim prayed that Allah would heal his mother and make her well.

His mother did not get well. She died following months of pain and distress. Salim was angry and could not understand how Allah could allow such a thing to happen.

Some time later Salim was explaining his feelings to his **imam**, who comforted him with compassionate words. The imam explained that in a very real sense Salim's mother had been made well – she had been made whole again, free from disease by the power of Allah, and she now enjoyed the beauty and tranquillity of Paradise.

Although it still hurt not to have his mother alive and with him, Salim understood what the imam meant. The life that Allah has given is more than a mortal existence on earth; it is eternal life. Sadly, at some stage, all mortal bodies die, but a person's spirit lives for ever.

The existence of Allah

In this section you will:

- understand the Muslim assertion that the statement 'Allah exists' is a statement of fact
- read about traditional arguments that have been put forward to demonstrate Allah's existence
- reflect upon the Muslim belief that Allah is perfect.

Moved by the power of Allah

Faith and trust

To be a true **Muslim** one must be able to proclaim the **faith** of the **shahadah**:

'Ash hadu an laa ilaha il-allahu wa Ash hada anna Muhammadar abduhu wa rasulu.'

(I believe there is no god but Allah; and I believe that Muhammad is the servant and messenger of Allah.)

For a Muslim to state 'I believe' indicates an acceptance of the reality of **Allah** in their hearts and minds.

'For all who profess the shahadah, Allah is as real as the beating of their own heart, He is the creator and sustainer of all things, there is no doubt of Allah's presence in the universe, no need to prove He exists.'

Imam Aurangzeb Khan

Arguments for the existence of Allah

For some people who are not Muslims the concept and existence of Allah can be difficult to understand and accept. For this reason Muslim scholars developed an argument to prove to all people that Allah must exist.

The 'Kalam argument' contends that:

- all things that exist have a cause
- it is impossible to go back forever looking for causes
- there must therefore have been a first cause, that was not caused itself
- Allah is the first cause as Allah is without cause and requires no explanation for His existence.

*The universe – the
work of Allah*

There are other possible arguments that could be put forward to demonstrate the fact of Allah's existence. For example, the fact that ever since the beginning of human history people have claimed to have experienced Allah may indicate the reality of Allah's presence in the universe.

Similarly, the world in which we live appears well ordered, as it sits in its orbit around the sun. Maybe the conditions for life on planet earth have been designed especially. If so there must have been a designer. This designer must have been Allah, the only power capable of such wonders.

In conclusion, the very fact that human beings have a sense of right and wrong and an understanding of what is meant by right and wrong must have come from somewhere. As children we have all made mistakes and have been guided by our parents – we have all been taught the correct way to behave. It is argued that this teaching and guidance must have come from Allah, the ultimate law giver and moral guide of all.

The perfection of Allah

'Allah is perfect, therefore, He exists.'

Muslims give Allah 99 different names – an attempt to express something of what they believe Allah to be like. However, these 99 names can only scratch the surface of Allah's nature. One thing is clear, however, from Allah's names: Muslims believe that Allah is perfect.

The fact that **Islam** teaches that Allah has all perfections can be used as a further argument that Allah must exist. Simply stated, to exist is in itself a perfection. Therefore, if Allah has all perfections, He must also possess the perfection of existence. Therefore, Allah must exist.

However, many would argue that existence is not a perfection, and here the argument fails. For Muslims, the success of this or any argument does not matter because the question of Allah's existence in simply a matter of faith and **trust**.

Glossary

Abd servant

Adhan the call to prayer

Akhirah belief in life after death

Allah God

Angel messenger from Allah, visible under certain conditions

Belief firm opinion, acceptance without doubt

Blasphemy acting or speaking disrespectfully about Allah

CE Common Era, dating from the year of the birth of 'Isa (pbuh)

Du'a personal prayer or supplication

Faith the courage to accept the challenges of belief

Hadiths sayings and traditions of Muhammad (pbuh)

Hajj annual pilgrimage to Makkah

Hajji name given to a Muslim man who has performed Hajj

Hajjah name given to a Muslim woman who has performed Hajj

Halal allowed

Hijab covering cloak worn by Muslim women

Ibadah worship, being a servant of God

Id-ul-Adha feast of sacrifice, ends the Hajj

Id-ul-Fitr feast to break the fast

Ihram state of religious 'separation' or purity

Imam a teacher or leader

Injil the revelation given to 'Isa (Jesus)

Islam submission to Allah

Istjfaa calling to prophethood

Jihad striving, holy war in defence of Allah's will

Jinn elemental spirit

Ka'bah the 'Cube', shrine of Allah in Makkah

Kalimah Tayyibah the last words spoken by a Muslim before dying

Khalifah deputy for Allah

Khitan circumcision

Khutbah sermon

Madrasah school

Mihrab niche indicating the direction of Makkah

Minaret tower from which the call to prayer is given

Minbar pulpit for giving Friday sermons

Mosque place for communal prayer and activities

Muslims followers of Islam

Pbuh 'Peace be upon him' (said of the prophets)

Prophets holy people, through whom Allah has revealed something of himself

Qur'an the Revealed Holy Book of Islam

Ramadan the month of fasting

Risalah prophecy

Sahifah of Ibrahim scrolls of Abraham and Moses

Salah ritual prayer five times daily

Sawm fasting from sunrise to sunset

Shahadah declaration of faith

Shaytan the Devil

Shirk sin of associating anything with Allah

Surah a chapter in the Qur'an

Tawhid the doctrine of the one-ness of Allah

Tawrah the revelation given to Musa (Moses) (pbuh)

Trust belief in the reliability or truth of something

Ummah the 'family' of Islam

Wudu ritual washing before prayer

Zabur the revelation given to Dawud (David) (pbuh)

Zakah giving of one-fortieth of savings for God's service

Places

Arafat Mount of Mercy, where Adam (pbuh) and Eve met after God forgave their sin

Jabal-un-Nur the Mountain of Light, where Muhammad (pbuh) regularly prayed in isolation in a cave

Makkah city of Ka'bah shrine, Muhammad's (pbuh) birthplace

Mina place of stoning the Devil on Hajj

Safa and **Marwah** places where Hajar searched for water

People

Abu Talib uncle of Muhammad (pbuh) who adopted him

Adam the first created man

Dawud the prophet David (pbuh), king of Israel

Fatimah daughter of Muhammad (pbuh)

Hajar wife of Ibrahim (pbuh)

Ibrahim Abraham, the 'father' of Jews and Arabs, and 'friend of God'

'Isa the prophet Jesus, worshipped by Christians

Isma'il the prophet Ishmael, son of Abraham

Jibril (Gabriel) the angel who transmitted revelations to Muhammad (pbuh)

Khadijah first wife of Muhammad (pbuh)

Muhammad the last and greatest of the prophets, to whom Allah revealed the Qu'ran

Musa the prophet Moses

Shaytan Satan, the devil, the chief Jinn

Suleiman the prophet Solomon, son of Dawud (David) (pbuh)

FALKIRK COUNCIL
LIBRARY SUPPORT
FOR SCHOOLS

Index